AF327135

Gladstone's
Boswell

For Frank and Kitty

'He told Mr Mill that he had never witnessed such
complete and contented idleness as in Corfu.'

Gladstone's Boswell
Late Victorian Conversations

by Lionel A. Tollemache
and other documents

Introduced and Edited by

Asa Briggs

Provost, Worcester College, Oxford

THE HARVESTER PRESS · SUSSEX
ST. MARTIN'S PRESS · NEW YORK

First published in 1984 by
THE HARVESTER PRESS LIMITED
Publisher: John Spiers
16 Ship Street, Brighton, Sussex

and in the USA by
ST. MARTIN'S PRESS, INC.
175 Fifth Avenue, New York, NY 10010

British Library Cataloguing in Publication Data

Tollemache, Lionel A.
   Gladstone's Boswell. — [3rd ed.]
   1. Gladstone, W. E. (William Ewart)
   2. Prime ministers — Great Britain —
   Biography
   I. Title   II. Briggs, Asa
   941.081′092′4   DA563.4

ISBN 0-901759-71-6

ST. MARTIN'S PRESS
ISBN 0-312-32766-8
LCN 84-45206

Typeset in 8½/10 point Garamond by
Alacrity Phototypesetters, Banwell Castle, Weston-super-Mare
Printed in Great Britain by
Whitstable Litho Ltd, Whitstable, Kent

THE HARVESTER PRESS PUBLISHING GROUP
The Harvester Press Publishing Group comprises Harvester Press Limited
(chiefly publishing literature, fiction, philosophy, psychology, and science and
trade books), Harvester Press Microform Publications Limited (publishing in
microform unpublished archives, scarce printed sources, and indexes to these
collections) and Wheatsheaf Books Limited (a wholly independent company
chiefly publishing in economics, international politics, sociology and related social
sciences), whose books are distributed by The Harvester Press Limited and its
agencies throughout the world.

CONTENTS

LIST OF ILLUSTRATIONS

FOREWORD

I would like to thank Mr M.R.D. Foot, who sent me a copy of his interesting John Rylands Library Lecture of 16 October 1968 on 'Morley's Gladstone: A Reappraisal' and lent me Lord Rosebery's personal copy of *Talks with Mr. Gladstone*. I am also indebted to Dr Colin Matthew, editor of Gladstone's *Diaries*, for a number of Tollemache references in them, and for details of family history to Major-General E.D.H. Tollemache's book, printed in Ipswich: *The Tollemaches of Helmingham and Ham* (1949). A very early version of part of this introduction was given to the Oxford Gladstone Seminar arranged by Dr Matthew and my colleague Mr G.H.L. Le May. My colleague Dr Michael Winterbotham has guided me through several classical translations. Finally I have been immensely helped in identifying Tollemache reviews by Susan Hard. The search continues.

Asa Briggs
Worcester College, Oxford

MR. GLADSTONE LISTENING.

INTRODUCTION

'The worst of nearly all biographies,' said Gladstone, 'is that they contain hardly anything but praise.' They may, of course, have other defects. John Morley's three-volume *Life of Gladstone*, which appeared in 1903, is still regarded – and rightly so – as magisterial, yet it excludes much that we would now consider essential for an understanding of the subject. Before Morley started on his massive task, contemporaries could be more sweeping about the inadequacies of his qualifications than we would be. Thus, in 1898 Sir Arthur Godley, formerly Gladstone's secretary, who had been approached to write the life before Morley accepted the assignment, told Sir Edward Hamilton, author of the first memoir of Gladstone to be published after his death, that 'to choose J. Morley to write Mr G.'s life is ... very much like choosing a man who has been blind from his birth, but is a clever writer, to do the biography of Millais or Burne Jones.'

Gladstone died on 19 May 1898, aged eighty-eight, and Hamilton's *Mr. Gladstone: A Monograph* appeared with remarkable speed in November. Lionel Tollemache's *Talks with Mr. Gladstone* came out fortuitously, however, even sooner in June 1898. Hamilton, like Godley, had served as Gladstone's secretary, and he described in the introduction to his book how privileged he had been to know Mr Gladstone for nearly forty years and 'still more privileged to have been brought into the closest contact with him for a considerable time.'

Tollemache was not so privileged, although he had first talked to Gladstone as long ago as the 1850s, when he was an undergraduate at Balliol College, Oxford. He did not share Gladstone's political views, and their usual *rendez-vous* was not, as in the case of Hamilton, an office, a club, a house or the House of Commons, but a hotel – and a French hotel in Biarritz at that. None the less, or perhaps because of this, *Talks with Mr. Gladstone*, the edited record of a number of conversations, which the *St James's Gazette* chose as 'the most interesting book of the year', is very special reading about Gladstone, particularly the aged Gladstone who liked to return in conversation, as many old men do, to his lost youth and middle age.

Morley was to be told by the Gladstone family not to attempt to survey Gladstone's religious life in any detail. Indeed, their views on religion were further apart than Gladstone's and Tollemache's on politics. By contrast, Tollemache loved not only conversation about theology (and the bearing upon it of science) but about the bases of morality. He was prepared to test Gladstone on every kind of subject, therefore, except the other subject on which Morley did not touch – Gladstone's long continued efforts to rescue London prostitutes from the streets, a subject which figures prominently in his *Diaries*, now at last in the course of well edited publication. The *Diaries*, indeed, present an intimate picture of a private Gladstone which it is impossible to secure from any other sources. We learn more, too, from them about the Gladstone family than it has ever been possible to know before, the family which took the decisions about the 'official' biography and biographer.

Talks with Mr. Gladstone, dedicated to Gladstone's daughter, Mary Drew, covers many of the same themes as Hamilton's *Mr. Gladstone, A Monograph*: indeed, it is closer to this graceful book than to the magisterial Morley. It was Hamilton who wrote of Gladstone,

The personal fascination of the man was so great that it could only be properly understood by those who were brought into social contact with him. One had to stand close by him – to 'go behind-scenes' – in order to appreciate in full the dexterity of the magician's wand. The moment one came into his near presence, one felt the peculiar spell.

Morley felt the spell, of course, and somewhat to his own political disadvantage, as his biographer D.A. Hamer shows, became what Gladstone called 'a main prop to me'. 'It is not the common lot of man,' Gladstone had told him in 1890, 'to make serious additions to the friendships which so greatly help us in this pilgrimage, after seventy-six years old; but I rejoice to think that in your case it has been accomplished for me.'

Tollemache's relationship with Gladstone, limited and fragmented though it was, had been far easier. His father, John Tollemache, created first Baron Tollemache of Helmingham in 1876, was an old friend of Gladstone and, although a strong Tory Protectionist, an old friend also of John Bright, with whom he was often seen walking arm-in-arm in the West End of London. He died in 1890, and Gladstone acquired and lived for a time in his London house (now Chatham House, headquarters of the Royal Institute of International Affairs, where three Prime Ministers have lived). Lionel wrote an interesting article about his father in the *Fortnightly Review* in 1892, which Gladstone described as 'charming' (see Appendix V). John's reminiscences introduced Lionel to the world of Wellington and Peel, and it was through his father that he first met Gladstone while an undergraduate.

Lionel described himself as 'a staunch Whig', whereas his father was a committed Tory who thought the Reform Bill of 1832 a necessary evil at best, and who voted against the repeal of the Corn Laws. He had sat as Member of Parliament for Cheshire South from 1841 to 1868, and for Cheshire West from 1868 to 1872, to be succeeded by his eldest son Wilbraham; and, while he had often taken young Lionel to hear debates at Westminster, the political difference between them held back Lionel's own political opportunities within the family. Parodoxically, as Lionel noted, time produced strange new patterns of thought and feeling. Joseph Chamberlain, not prone to flattery, described the first Baron as one of the very best of English landlords, and it was after visiting his estates (where there were allotments for farm labourers) that Impey wrote his pamphlet *Three Acres and a Cow*, a key-point in Chamberlain's unauthorised radical programme of 1885. Lionel, like Gladstone, had no sympathy with 'constructive' radicalism of this kind, with 'the odd result', as he put it, that his father, 'at the end of his active and useful life, seemed to be in some respects less out of sympathy with modern Liberalism than I was.'

There was another family reason which brought Lionel close to Gladstone. His wife Beatrix, whom he married in 1870, was the youngest daughter of William Tatton Egerton, Baron Egerton of Tatton, and the Egertons were Cheshire neighbours and friends of the Gladstones. A few months before meeting Gladstone at Biarritz in 1891 – after an interval of more than twenty years – Tollemache had written to him enclosing a copy of his book of essays, *Stones of Stumbling*, and some verses written by himself and his wife. Beatrix, who knew and liked Catherine Gladstone, was something of a poet, who wrote poems with titles like 'The Child's Song' and 'Rest and Unrest – Handel and Beethoven': the *Oxford Magazine* described her *Engelberg and Other Verses* as 'the garnered visions of a woman who walks the world with serious joy.' In the conversations with Gladstone, Beatrix played her part: 'both she and I paid great attention to his remarks; and my report of them, which was drawn up at the earliest opportunity, was carefully revised by her.' At the same time, partly but not entirely because of these family reasons, Gladstone did not choose to say much about the immediate 'politics of the day' to either of them: 'he seldom approached burning questions in my presence and hardly ever in the presence of my wife.' There was talk about past politics, but they stopped at Parnell, and even in this case Tollemache, for the only time in his book, put in a few dots, with the explanation that 'a phrase' had been omitted which he was 'assured did not express Mr Gladstone's deliberate opinion.'

Tollemache was right to express only qualified regret that immediate politics, the far from easy politics of the 1890s, were left out. 'The political Gladstone has long been and will continue to be in everybody's mouth. It is of the non-political Gladstone that people in general need to learn something.' Appendix IV presents a picture of the public Gladstone of the 1890s, the Grand Old Man, as drawn by one of the most experienced political journalists of the day – Frank Harrison Hill, editor of the *Daily News* from 1869 to 1886. Tollemache's picture is very different.

From the start he broached religion. The reason why he had not published *Stones of Stumbling* earlier, he told Gladstone in his letter of 2 March 1891, was that he knew that it would offend 'the extreme Evangelicalism of my father'.

Gladstone would have appreciated such a reference and such a reason – a reason which Tollemache never made public. He replied at once, and soon there was further correspondence on 'the failure of the Oxford [theological] Liberals' to appreciate Bishop Butler. This was one of the most congenial of all themes to Gladstone: he had been fascinated by Butler since he was an undergraduate, spent hours planning an edition of Butler with related essays, and took up the problems in some of his last letters to the Duke of Argyll after his retirement from politics in 1894. Tollemache quickly switched to another religious theme close to both Gladstone and himself. In a second letter, written nine days after the first, he told Gladstone that a priest at Brompton Oratory had complimented him on showing more 'insight into Catholicism' than any non-Catholic he had ever met. Gladstone was always willing to discuss with friends Manning, and further back in time the Oxford Movement.

Stones of Stumbling was one of a pair of volumes of essays, many of which had been published before – sometimes in less finished and extended form – in the *Fortnightly Review*, the great Liberal periodical, founded in 1865, which Morley had edited from 1868 to 1882. The other volume was called *Safe Studies*, to distinguish the contents of the collection from the 'dangerous' (i.e. theologically or philosophically dangerous) contents of some of Tollemache's other writing. Both volumes appeared for sale 'at cost price' in 1891, although they had previously been printed for private circulation, and in this form had made their way to the British Museum and other great libraries. The Preface to *Safe Studies* was regarded by Tollemache as an *apologia pro scriptis meis*. This was easy and familiar Latin, but it was perhaps a sign of the times that a note to the fourth edition (1895) reads 'As non-classical readers have often complained of being baffled by my classical quotations, I have thought it better in bringing out a new edition of my volumes to subjoin an Index, with translations.'

The two volumes of essays were very well received. The *Saturday Review*, which did not share Tollemache's opinions, gave 'hearty praise' to both: 'his work has the literary flavour throughout, without being merely bookish, and he can argue a thesis like a craftsman and master of his craft.' *The Times* discovered 'literary merit of a high and rare order'. *The Speaker* said in language which echoes decades later, 'his truly marvellous memory for details of speech and character may keep for us many a little trait, or passing word, which will hereafter be precious.' The *Scotsman* gave a further reason why these two volumes, little known, should be read by all historians who are interested in the changing Victorian frame of mind; 'they give in an agreeable form an outline or suggestion of all that has been most prominent and characteristic for the past twenty or thirty years in the leading currents of speculative thought in England.'

I read these two volumes after I read *Talks with Mr. Gladstone*, and they clearly point the way forward to what is still – if only on account of its subject – Tollemache's most interesting book. Moreover, they point the way not only to the themes but to the method. In particular, a series of dialogue recollections of characters as different as Mark Pattison and Sir Charles Wheatstone introduces us to Tollemache the catechist. The *Guardian* already said of these early essays that he revealed himself as 'a worthy follower of Boswell', and he himself was to say more of his 'Boswellian canons' in the preface to *Talks*. His obituary in *The Times* in 1919 was to be headed 'A Boswell of Many Friends'.

The technique of the interview is not a product of a radio age: Tollemache understood it well, knowing when to probe and when to persuade, although he had a bad stammer which would have halted him before a microphone or a camera. He asked the right question in his preface to *Talks*: 'in order to concentrate on the portrait itself ought not its frame to be as simple as possible?' Curiously, he used the word 'broadcast' in the Preface to *Safe Studies*: he had been persuaded by friends, he said, to tell his stories broadcast to a wider public. Critics at the time, of course, could not see into the radio age even with the benefit of Tollemache's interesting essay on historical prediction. They rather looked backward to Boswell in the eighteenth century and in more recent times, Abraham Hayward (1801-84), now even less frequently read or referred to than Tollemache, although, unlike Tollemache, he has an entry in the *Dictionary of National Biography*. Hayward, whom Tollemache had met, contributed regularly to the *Quarterly Review* and other periodicals and less frequently to *The Times*: he also published three volumes of essays, and a selection of his correspondence appeared in 1886. In its review of *Safe Studies* and *Stones for Stumbling* the *Daily Chronicle* tried to establish a nineteenth-century perspective: 'Since the death of Hayward,' the reviewer wrote, 'we know no English *littérateur* who has in the same degree as Mr. Tollemache the happy knack of recollecting or connecting the characteristic sayings and doings of a distinguished man, and piecing them together in a finished mosaic.' Tollemache was 'ready for Gladstone' in 1891. Already he knew how to dissect experience and to liberate speculation. Already, too, he knew the power of an anecdote, recognising realistically that 'what are chestnuts to the few are nuts to the many.'

American readers loved both the 'nutty' and 'fruity' quality of his books, which were equally well received on both sides of the Atlantic. Long before G.M. Young wrote his brilliant essay *Victorian England, Portrait of an Age*, an essay which can be re-read with profit and delight time and time again, a reviewer in the American periodical *Book Chat* said of Tollemache that he had 'the rare gift of being able to paint portraits instead of making photographs, and he has cultivated this now almost lost art until it has reached perfection.' He himself, as we have seen, used the same language when he talked of a portrait and its frame, although he had one lapse when he said that his function was to produce an ethograph of Gladstone – a photograph of his 'moral and social physiognomy'.

The frame was certainly sturdy enough. So it was too in a series of recollections of Benjamin Jowett, formidable Master of Balliol, which Tollemache published in the *Journal of Education* in 1895, when *Talks with Mr. Gladstone* was already well advanced. It was appropriate that, already having 'dealt with' Pattison, he should turn to Jowett, careful though he was to avoid choosing between them (as so many writers have done since). Samples of his dialogues with Jowett are given in Appendix I. In a letter to Gladstone in October 1895, Tollemache described Jowett over-simply as 'the typical Platonist' and Pattison as 'the typical Aristotelian'.

A few reviewers were less sure of the metaphors of the picture and frame. The *Daily Telegraph* preferred those of wine and goatskin. 'There is a certain Spanish wine with a peculiar flavour, as to the origin of which conoisseurs – whether they like it or not – are disagreed. Some hold that it is due to the grape from which the wine with a peculiar flavour, as to the origin of which connoisseurs – whether they earlier stages.' The *Telegraph* complained that in *Talks with Mr. Gladstone* there was too much Tollemache goatskin, and too little Gladstone wine. This too, of course, is a matter of taste. To me, the *Telegraph* was wrong.

One reason why *Talks with Mr. Gladstone* is a favourite book of mine is that I am in broad sympathy with G.M. Young's view that what matters most in history is not what happened, but what people said about it when it was happening – 'about it and round about it, because after all very little of any man's time is spent in talking about the things that get into the history books.' For this reason, it is illuminating to study Tollemache alongside C.R.L. Fletcher's *Mr. Gladstone at Oxford* which, though not published until 1908, dealt with a visit of Gladstone to Oxford in 1890 during which he stayed in Young's old college, All Souls. Fletcher was a conscientious recorder of what he called 'the extraordinary volume and vivacity of Mr Gladstone's talk' (a sample of dialogue is given in Appendix II); and he was writing his book late enough to win the approval of Morley, who told him that 'he was convinced that the more that is known about Mr. Gladstone the greater he will appear.' One of Fletcher's colleagues wrote that 'the charm of his [Gladstone's] talk cannot be rendered in description – the softness of the lower tones of the voice, the easy constant movement as he turned from one to the other: the clenched fist, the open palm, and the challenging forefinger, which the House of Commons knew so well.'

The Times reviewer of Tollemache's book maintained first that 'there is a great deal to be gathered from such talk which helps us to realise what the great men of the past were like', and second that 'Mr Tollemache has set forth his recollections with discretion as well as skill.' He did not dwell on what he meant by discretion, although some of the Fellows of All Souls knew well enough how important it was in talking to Gladstone to steer away from certain items of conversation which provoked 'a momentary and very characteristic lifting of that well-known right eyebrow'. 'Mr Gladstone's chief characteristic in conversation,' *The Times* reviewer went on, was 'his intense earnestness on every subject', 'well hit off in the epigrammatic remark made long ago by one of his friends that he would talk about a piece of old china as if he were standing before the judgment seat of God.' Tollemache echoed this, he went on, when he spoke of 'the particularly inelastic and stereotyped earnestness of manner which made it hard sometimes to tell whether Mr. Gladstone was speaking on a grave or a light topic', and added that although his talk was not rhetorical, it was emphatically the talk of an orator. 'However, it was nearly always extremely interesting talk and the conversations here are very good reading.'

And that is a second reason why this is a favourite book of mine. The talk is almost always interesting even when it strays far away from the main pre-occupations of the period. It ranges over as many topics and anecdotes as Harold Macmillan's talk, famous in our own time and over as long a time-span. It covers books as much as people, and it is packed with significant allusions and assessments. In his appendix to *Stones of Stumbling*, Tollemache had described the dying Pattison asking for some of *his* favourite volumes, stroking them lovingly, and pondering whether he will have his books in Heaven.

There is a strong Oxford flavour to *Talks with Mr. Gladstone*, who, in his own words, delivered in the Union, 'loved every stone in its walls.' Gladstone presented himself to many dons in Oxford 'as an Oxford man who had gone into the Liberal party because the Tory party was under – *influences*': he valued Oxford 'as the power counteracting dangerous tendencies in politics'. Tolle-mache was proud that he first met him when he was canvassing the Oxford electors in 1857. Gladstone never reached the heights of the Chancellorship, as Harold Macmillan has done, but as Member of Parliament for the University from 1847 to 1865 he was deeply devoted to University and College ways of life. On his visits to Oxford in 1890 and at other times – his last visit was in 1892 to deliver the first Romanes Lecture – he impressed most dons who met him by his adherence to what were then regarded as somewhat outmoded features of College and University life. 'His own political supporters, good academic Liberals,' Fletcher wrote, 'were expected to sympathise with views about the University which dated from 1847 at the latest.'

In Gladstone's last illness the Hebdomadal Council of the University was to send him a message of sorrow and affection, referring to the 'no ordinary bond' which linked him with it, and Morley himself had been deeply impressed in 1892 – around the very time Gladstone was talking to Tollemache – with 'his solicitude for the well-being and right-doing of Oxford and Cambridge, the two eyes of the country.' 'This connection between the higher education and the general movement of the national mind', Morley went on, 'engages his profound attention, and no doubt deserves such attention in any statesman, who looks beyond the mere surface problems of the day.' Morley had no doubt about the moral, which he had urged himself during the 1870s: 'to perceive the bearings of such matters as these, makes Mr. G. a statesman of the highest class, as distinguished from men of clever expedients.'

Yet Gladstone liked gossip about Oxford as much as high-sounding statements about its role in national life. Little things about it interested him as much as big things, though some of the little things were often endowed with bigger social and cultural significance. He must have surprised the Chairman of Oxford's Liberal 'Three Hundred', for instance, by claiming that not only Christ Church, his old college, but the University as a whole had suffered as a result of the disappearance of 'our noblemen and gentlemen commoners'. It should be added that when Lord Salisbury was told of this statment he remarked drily that 'when these privileged persons existed, Mr. Gladstone was always urging their abolition.'

It should perhaps be added too that Lord Salisbury would never have found himself walking along the High Street in full academic dress (complete with umbrella) and being saluted by lined-up cabmen doffing their hats. Gladstone, however, took such adulation in his stride. One day he arrived at breakfast in All Souls carrying a brown loaf presented to him by a baker who 'was pleased to describe himself as an admirer'. After eating it, Gladstone gave 'a full account of its merits' and went on to generalise about his admirers: their 'operations', he said, reduced themselves 'on the average and in the long run to a kind of balance: some of them present me with things which they suppose I want and others steal what I have.' This is a realistic rather than cynical remark, as a *Daily Graphic* article of October 1890 on Gladstone's Hawarden home reveals – 'Although the general behaviour of those who annually visit Hawarden is excellent, yet the natural consequence is the gradual disappearance of ferns and plants which can easily be removed. Some unmannerly person even cut out Mr. Gladstone's name from his Bible in Church.'

The Fellows of All Souls found such gestures out of the question. They were alert, however, to the kind of 'contradictions' in Gladstone's character and attitudes which Salisbury commented upon. G.W.E. Russell, who quoted the *Daily Graphic* article in his *The Rt. Hon. W.E. Gladstone*, a short biography published in 1892, noted 'his natural bias to respect institutions as they are.' His favourite argument for Home Rule was that it was 'merely a return to the system of Government which commended it to our forefathers and which their presumptuous children heedlessly set aside.' Such conservatism, as the Fellows of All Souls realised, was not merely social. Hamilton referred both to his 'apparently inconsistent statements' and to his 'contrarieties of impulse'. Gladstone might be happy in All Souls – even agreeing with the Duke of Wellington's comment in 1830 that the Constitution was incapable of improvement – but he believed too in the counter-proposition that 'the immediate instincts and sense of the people were generally right.' He might defend the hereditary principle, particularly in face of what he thought of as 'plutocracy', yet his last speech in Parliament was a vigorous attack on the House of Lords, identifying a 'difference of fundamental tendency' between the two Houses, and arguing that 'it cannot continue'. He might claim, as he did in Oxford, that 'the English people are extraordinarily difficult to work up to excitement on any question', yet one of the main conservative grumbles against him was that he would not allow the people to be still. George Norman, 'last patriarch of Benthamism', whom Tollemache quoted in his article on his father (see Appendix V), once told him feelingly: 'I only wish that Gladstone would leave us without organic changes for the next forty years.'

Tollemache did not care about inconsistencies and contrarieties. In his 'Recollections of Pattison', he extolled the paradox: 'Woe to the man who does not contradict himself at least once a day.' He quoted Renan also, to the effect that *'presque tous nous sommes doubles'*. The furthest he would go in *Talks with Mr. Gladstone*, whom he recognised would never have appealed to Renan, was that 'he was subtle and even sophisticated in his explanations of his devious courses. Yet in giving these explanations he was perfectly sincere.' Tollemache associated certain kinds of inconsistency with tendencies to 'oratory' – an art of which he was intensely suspicious, but he remarked also that it was not only political opponents but Philistines who failed to appreciate certain kinds of oratorical gifts.

There is a marked difference in this respect between Tollemache and Morley. The latter, deeply moved by Gladstone's oratory and by Gladstone's own statements about it in one of his volumes of *Gleanings*, detected a profound coherence in everything Gladstone did: his 'genius was one'. The aim of his biography, therefore, was to 'present a picture of Mr. Gladstone showing that he was a whole man from the beginning to the end of his career, that one set of principles animated him from first to last, and that one set of objects promoted actions.' Tollemache wrote in his 'Recollections of Pattison' that 'biography is sometimes autobiography in disguise', and certainly, as Morley's own biographer points out, 'the kind of Gladstone presented in the *Life* is, in fact, very much the kind of man that Morley himself always wanted to be, able to bring diverse and fragmented interests into an organic unity of thought and action.'

Morley was not only recalling: he was wading with incredible speed through a mass of manuscript documentation. Tollemache, like the Oxford dons, was listening and comparing. The Fellows of All Souls found Gladstone easier to talk to – and to listen to – at breakfast. At dinner, 'although his talk was more sustained, it seemed to cost him a greater effort, and after nine o'clock he often yawned.' Yet they were a good audience, curious, alert and critical, and they went away from breakfast feeling that they had not been hearing a monologue, but participating in 'a conversation led and dominated by a master of the dialogue'. It was Gladstone, not Macmillan, however, who told such a group that an audience of actors was the best of audiences which he had ever experienced: they appreciated all his points with 'such rapidity'.

Tollemache, who met Gladstone at Biarritz mainly over dinner, had exceptional 'rapidity of response'. Moreover, he might have been a nobleman-commoner had he not been awarded one of the only two Balliol Scholarships in Classics after leaving Harrow in 1856. His family, whatever its Victorian (and earlier) idiosyncracies, has been described in this century by Field-Marshal Earl Wavell as 'one of the oldest in England', and the first Baron Tollemache would have warmed to his opinion that the family, Norman in origin (the American variant of the name was Talmage), had always 'had its roots firmly in the English countryside, living in the same home from generation to generation'.

Lionel himself described his father as 'the grandest specimen of a country gentleman that our generation has seen or is likely to see.' None the less, he was only too aware that on grounds of health, he himself was 'forced to spend three-quarters of every year on the Continent in a sort of valetudinarian exile'. He had an accident as a child which left him slightly lame, and his eyesight was even weaker than his general constitution. He sometimes spoke, as to Gladstone, of his 'near-blindness', and for many years before his death he was completely blind. In his *Who's Who* entry he stated under 'recreations', always one of the most revealing entries, 'debarred by extreme near-sightedness from ordinary amusements; hearing poetry and novels read aloud, and studying human nature': it is quite astonishing that he knew so much about books.

In one sense, the encounters between Tollemache and Gladstone at Biarritz were encounters between the blind and the deaf, for the Oxford dons of 1890 had commented as much upon Gladstone's deafness as upon his Lancashire accent. By 1896, moreover, the date of the last Tollemache interviews, his eyesight was weakening too. Fortunately, both men were in full possession of their mental faculties. Long after Gladstone's death, Sir George Trevelyan was to recall that Gladstone's gifts and faculties were 'exactly a whole generation better than his time of life', and Tollemache, not yet sixty (he was born in 1838) was to outlive the first world war.

*   *   *

Gladstone visited Biarritz in 1891, 1892, 1893, 1894 and 1895-6. On each occasion he travelled there with his friend George Armitstead, the rich bachelor, Liberal Member of Parliament for Dundee from 1868–73 and 1880–5. He has been described as Gladstone's unofficial travel agent, but he was close enough to him for him to serve as one of the pall-bearers at Gladstone's funeral. (Lord Rosebery was another, and two members of the Royal family also served, to the Queen's distaste – the Prince of Wales and the Duke of York).

On the first of these Biarritz visits Morley was a member of Gladstone's party, and he has left an interesting account – some of it as catechistic in presentation as Tollemache's (see Appendix III): Chapter VI of Book X of his *Life* is called 'Biarritz', with page titles that include 'table-talk', 'use of epigrams' and 'opinions on statesmen'. There are no cross-references, however, to Tollemache, just as there are no cross-references in Tollemache to Morley. 23 December 1891, when Tollemache dined with Armitstead and the Gladstones, is not one of the dates mentioned by Morley, although he has entries for the days before and after.

There is an entry for 2 January 1892, the day when the Gladstones dined with the Tollemaches, but it ends with a visit to Bayonne in the afternoon. It is extremely interesting to compare the conversations of this obviously busy day with Morley ending by paying Gladstone lavish compliments: 'I have many a time seen him in London and at Hawarden not far from trivial. But here at Biarritz all is appropriate ... He can be playful and gay as youth', but 'he cannot resist rising in an instant to the general point of view – to grasp the elemental considerations of character, history, belief, conduct, affairs.' And on this occasion it was Morley who brought in Mark Pattison: 'It is not his knowledge that attracts; it is not his ethical tests and standards; it is not that dialectical strength of arm which, as Mark Pattison said of him, could twist a bar of iron to its purpose. It is the combination of these with elevation, with true sincerity, with extraordinary mental force.'

After so much talking on 2 January, Gladstone must surely have been confirmed in his 'only complaint against Biarritz' – that the society was too exclusively English. (He had heard an English preacher, doubtless the Rev. W.G. Sharpin on Christmas Day, a preacher 'with a great command of his art'.) At this time Biarritz was a town of less than 10,000 inhabitants, 'especially frequented', as Baedeker put it in 1895, 'by the upper classes, by the aristocracy of Southern France and by Spaniards in summer, and by the English in winter'. Gladstone stayed at the Grand Hotel which, with its seven gates, immediately brought Homer to his mind. Tollemache stayed at the Hotel d'Angleterre. Both hotels overlooked the beach, and Gladstone loved the sound of 'the swell of the mighty bay': as Morley said, he had 'a passion for the sound of the sea; would like to have it in his ear all day and night.' On his second visit to Biarritz – this time without Morley – Tollemache's first entry for 2 January 1892 reads 'Mr Gladstone never saw such a grand sea and such sheets of foam as on the shores of Biarritz, and he thought that, if Tennyson had seen it, he would have written about it.'

Tollemache did not mention that Gladstone was now Prime Minister again. He had formed his fourth and last administration in August 1892 and just before going to Biarritz he had been working on the heads of a new Home Rule Bill. (Another event of 1892 had been that a fortnight after he had taken office a heifer had knocked him down in Hawarden Park.) There seem to have been no discussions on recent politics on this occasion, although Gladstone had told Tollemache the previous year not only that Home Rule would soon be carried, but that people would eventually have difficulty in understanding the state of mind which postponed the carrying of it for so long. In the interval, Gladstone had sent the Queen what she considered a 'very curious document', warning that 'the longer the struggle is continued, the more the Liberal party will verge towards democratic opinion.' This was a threat, not a promise. The new Home Rule Bill was introduced on 13 February 1893 just over a month after Gladstone had returned refreshed from Biarritz, and a month later Gladstone sent Tollemache with 'no apology' a collection of his writings on Ireland.

There was no further meeting between them until late January 1894, although 'a learned divine', who lived near Biarritz, furnished Gladstone with notes of a conversation which took place soon after Gladstone's arrival there a few days before. Ireland figured in this conversation, with Gladstone reiterating his view that the Irish had done nothing to warrant the English oppression: 'they were only reclaiming that of which they had been gratuitously deprived.' Business connected with the Home Rule Bill had taken the whole of the previous year, with the House of Lords throwing the measure out in September. Thereafter there was confusion as Gladstone resisted pressure inside his own Cabinet to increase the naval estimates. When he left for Biarritz, later than he would have hoped – this year he had to spend his birthday (29 December) in England – he told Rosebery, whose Liberal Imperialist views were diametrically opposed to his own – that the great dead were with him – Peel, Cobden, Bright, Aberdeen and that the Admirals with whom he was contending were all mad. There were many people, however, who believed that it was Gladstone who was mad, and Rosebery recalled a prophecy of Palmerston that Gladstone would wreck the Liberal party and die in a madhouse. Given this extraordinary background, the two early 1894 conversations between Gladstone and Tollemache come as something of an anticlimax. They end, however, with Gladstone telling Tollemache: 'Your memory makes you formidable, but you are so good-natured that one does not feel afraid of you.'

Gladstone was only too conscious in 1894 of the presence around him of 'formidable' men, even if in his opinion they were intellectually and morally inferior to the generation before them. On 3 March 1894 he was to retire from political leadership. This time, it was Morley who found the right words – Matthew Prior's lines, quoted by Gladstone's favourite, Sir Walter Scott:

> The man in graver tragic known,
> (Though his best part long since was done)
> Still on the stage desires to tarry ... ,
> Unwilling to retire, though weary.

There were many Liberals who thought his retirement came too late. 'I cannot help wishing,' Sir George Trevelyan wrote later, 'that he had retired from office long before he did and had allowed the Liberal party to work out its own salvation, make its own mistakes, and learn from its own experience.'

The last talks between Tollemache and Gladstone took place in January 1896.

Gladstone had left England for Biarritz and Cannes on 28 December 1895 and the four conversations between them – one was at tea – were as broad-ranging as any in the series. Tollemache tried, indeed, to steer the second conversation – or at least the second which he recorded – towards safer topics than they were considering – death and immortality were certainly dangerous – yet Gladstone himself turned their course 'away from the smooth water and steered straight towards the Day of Judgment.'

This would have made a good ending to the volume, but for some reason Tollemache chose to break his usual chronological sequence and include a dinner conversation of 8 January after conversations of 13 and 18 January (or is this a mistake in the text?). Even then he did not choose a punch-line from it: what could have been more telling than Gladstone's 'melancholy observation': 'Nowhere does the ideal enter so little as into politics; nowhere does human conduct fall so far below the highest ethical standard. I did not always think this; but I am convinced of it now'? As it was, Tollemache obtained Gladstone's final blessing on 8 February, and ended his volume with two lines from Ovid.

Gladstone went on from Biarritz to Cannes. After meeting the Queen at Cimiez – she gave him her hand for the first time in their long relationship – he felt that *her* 'peculiar faculty and habit of conversation had disappeared'. He could be as hard as she was, and he added unfairly that 'it was a faculty, not so much the free offspring of a rich and powerful mind, as the fruit of assiduous care with long practice and much opportunity.' He had never been short of either practice or opportunity himself.

He had one more visit to Cannes to the home of his other great friend who loved to visit France, Lord Rendel, in November 1897, but it was at Hawarden that he died on 19 May 1898, Ascension Day. The last persons outside his own household to see him were Morley and Rosebery, representatives of two very different kinds of family, representatives of two very different kinds of Liberalism. Many honours followed. It was the experienced biographer, Sir Wemyss Reid, writing with the very active help of Francis Hirst, later to edit the *Economist*, who caught the mood best in his biography of Gladstone published four years before Morley's: 'Only to the greatest of the heroes of our national story have honours been rendered at their death such as fell to the lot of Mr. Gladstone; and upon none, be he warrior, or statesman, or poet, or philanthropist, was higher honour ever bestowed.'

*   *   *

Tollemache, who talked to Gladstone about warriors, statesmen, poets and philanthropists, did not treat Gladstone as a hero. It is true that he first approached him with a kind of 'religious awe', and that he ended his encounters with the thought, not finally demonstrated, that he deserved the title 'Holy Father of thy Country'. None the less, Tollemache took none of Gladstone's own thoughts as necessarily true or profound. On one occasion he could refer to Bagehot, and remark 'without disrespect' that some of Gladstone's sayings illustrated his dictum that 'a constitutional statesman is in general a man of common opinions and uncommon abilities – of the powers of a first-rate man and the creed of a second-rate man.' Tollemache may have been thinking of the creed more than of the opinions. Yet he was influenced by Bagehot's suspicion of 'the oratorical impulse' as a disorganising impulse: 'the higher faculties of the mind require a certain calm, and the excitement of oratory is unfavourable to that calm.'

His views are best set out in an essay on physical and moral courage printed in *Safe Studies*; but even in *Talks* he quotes a witness hostile to Gladstone who claimed that his 'vehement, and so to say apocalyptic, use of language, showed a certain want of moral perspective.' Every writer on Gladstone had pages or paragraphs to write on Gladstone's oratory, some finding it majestic, others verbose. All noticed its occasional repetition, its frequent obscurity. Tollemache himself was not entirely happy about his style in private conversatio, where, as these *Talks* reveal, he was neither repetitive nor obscure. 'It was not through rounded sentences,' Tollemache observed, 'nor through a spouting, and, so to say, rounded delivery, but through the frequent use of strong phrases, vocally italicised, and perhaps, I should add, through the not infrequent accumulation of nearly synonymous epithets when perhaps a single epithet would have sufficed, that the note of the orator was discernible in his discourse.'

Since Tollemache believed that the 'spiritual fire' of the orator could be too much for him, he believed, too, that orators, like artists and unlike mathematicians, were liable to early mortality: they could waste away 'like jelly on a hot plate'. Palmerston he did not feel to be an exception. Indeed, it was because Palmerston was free from 'the oratorical vexation of spirit', he felt, 'that he continued Prime Minister of a great nation at an age unsurpassed except by Fleury, whose political longevity Lord Palmerston spoke of with a sort of envy.'

Part of the hidden interest of these conversations is that Tollemache was fascinated by longevity. The early pages of the *Talks* are far less interesting than the later pages which are introduced, appropriately enough, with a glance at the *Winter's Tale*: 'Our scene is transferred from England to Biarritz at the same time that our drama overleaps a score of years.' We leave Gladstone in his forties and fifties, and rediscover him in his eighties.

One of the most curious essays in *Safe Studies* has the title 'Sir George Cornewall Lewis and Longevity' which hovers happily around the borderlands of history and medicine. Persons who live to ninety or a hundred, said Tollemache in the 1860s, have generally had better health at fifty than persons who die at sixty or sixty-five – this must have been one of the safest remarks he ever made:

'where we suppose a prolonged life, we must suppose also a prolonged youth.' There are other passages in his essay, however, which anticipate Sir Francis Galton, who wanted people to keep 'trees of life', recording their own medical histories and those of their ancestors, relatives and descendants. Tollemache had more interesting family material at his disposal than any that might have been offered by Gladstone, for his father, who married twice, had no fewer than twenty-four sons (of whom only twelve survived him) but only one daughter. His first wife was his first cousin and 'in loyalty to her', we are told, he not only insisted on wearing a band of crêpe around his hat at his second wedding, but took young Lionel, then aged eleven, with them on their honeymoon. We are not so much hovering around the borderlands of psychology here as reaching its core. It perhaps should be added, however, that four of the sons by the second marriage were in the Eton eleven, and a fifth was twelfth man.

The rather critical review of *Talks with Mr. Gladstone* – and it was exceptional in this – complained that there was more Tollemache in the book than there should have been. In fact, Tollemache's own interests enliven rather than weaken the interest, and the *Daily Telegraph* itself made no such complaints about his *Benjamin Jowett* when it appeared three years earlier (although the *Edinburgh Review* did). It was because Tollemache was more interested in science than Gladstone – he had been fascinated by Charles Babbage, and called Wheatstone's electro-magnetic telegraph 'the most marvellous of all modern inventions' – that he pressed Gladstone on scientific topics. They exchanged letters on the steam-engine, and in *Talks* Gladstone said, rather surprisingly, that science would be 'the great instrument of education in the future'. When he was pressed, however, to comment on the relative sums used to endow scientific research in England and Germany, he quickly shifted the subject to the public schools, and his conviction that Eton was 'more expensive now than it was in his younger days and that Harrow was more expensive still.' The expense was, of course, in his view well worth while: 'it would be like knocking a front tooth out of our English social life' if the public school system were to go, Fletcher noted, when Gladstone was at All Souls, that he remembered even more about Eton than about Oxford; and he told Fletcher that 'the public school system is the greatest thing in England, not even excepting the House of Lords.' Science was not once mentioned in Oxford.

Another subject of interest to Tollemache, which evoked little response from Gladstone, was 'the shape of the future'. Tollemache himself felt that his essay on historical prediction in *Safe Studies* made 'stiff reading'. Yet he doubtless expected a rather different answer from Gladstone to his question 'Are you not inclined to take a thoroughly snaguine view of the prospects of this very reforming age?' from the one that he got: 'Not altogether. The future is to me a blank. I cannot guess at all what is coming.' Further questioning revealed at least that Gladstone was not 'sanguine'. He went on to identify two dark shapes in the

future associated with plutocracy and militarism. He regretted 'the era of great
fortunes' in England, looking anxiously across the Atlantic, and 'the era of great
armament'; yet looking less anxiously across the Channel, when Tollemache
specifically mentioned the possibility of the huge German army attacking the
small British army, Gladstone replied that he was not in the least afraid. He put his
own question to Tollemache: 'How are they to cross the Channel without ships?
They would get very wet.' Tollemache put the last sentence into italics, a very rare
example of his directing attention to a particular Gladstone phrase.

   There are some other interesting exchanges on foreign attitudes towards
Britain and the devastatingly simple statement picked up in most of the reviews:
'The idea that the colonies add to the strength of the mother country appears to
me to be as dark a superstition as any that existed in the Middle Ages.'

   Joseph Chamberlain was then Colonial Secretary in Salisbury's Unionist
administration, and the country was within striking distance of the traumas of
the Boer Wars. Rosebery, too, whose political differences with Gladstone had
been very marked during Gladstone's last Cabinet, was proud to be thought of as
a Liberal Imperialist. The Liberal Imperialists were very unhappy about the
choice of Morley as Gladstone's biographer, and they cannot have been happy to
read of many of Gladstone's opinions as expressed in *Talks*. Rosebery himself
had been asked to write a 'character sketch' of him by the family.

   Rosebery's own annotated copy of *Talks with Mr. Gladstone* survives. He put
an exclamation mark against Gladstone's comment that the Franco-German
War was 'almost entirely the act of the Emperor'; and alongside Tollemache's
references to Gladstone's interest in china, he wrote in his most critical gloss:
'reputed to have been an enthusiastic ignoramus about china. His collection
realised very little.' Against one of Tollemache's leading questions of his own to
himself – 'How came it about that this conspicuously upright and conscientious
statesman was so grievously misunderstood?' – he jotted 'a difficult question to
answer'. It was a question that haunted Rosebery. He read Tollemache twice, and
there are two general notes in his hand on the volume as a whole. The first, dated
June 1898, reads 'The record of Tollemache's views is very interesting. So are the
occasional glimpses of Mr. Gladstone.' The second, dated July 1914 – an
interesting date – reads 'A harsh judgment. There are some striking things in this
book.'

   The 'striking things' are often as striking today as they were in 1898 or in 1914.
When asked about a possible 'yellow peril', Gladstone replied simply, 'If the
cultivated races cannot defend themselves without appealing to brute force, God
help them.' On another occasion: 'I used to think the Irish the most oppressed
people on earth, but I now think that the Jews have been even more oppressed.'
He liked to collect Basque proverbs and British paradoxes: 'he expressed a wish',
on one occasion, that 'modern Conservatives had a greater love of antiquity'.
'Would you have women made professors?' Tollemache demanded. 'There

might be certain difficulties about that,' Gladstone replied. 'We seem to be unpopular all over the world,' he also said. 'Now, when an individual is disliked by all his neighbours, one naturally asks whether he has not done something to deserve his own unpopularity.' Few Victorians, even the most critical, would have put this proposition quite in this very unverbose, but characteristically Gladstonian, way.

TALKS

WITH

MR. GLADSTONE

BY THE

HON. LIONEL A. TOLLEMACHE

AUTHOR OF
"BENJAMIN JOWETT" "SAFE STUDIES" ETC.

THIRD REVISED EDITION

Defunctus adhuc loquitur

LONDON
EDWARD ARNOLD
1903

TO

MARY DREW

THIS VOLUME IS AFFECTIONATELY DEDICATED BY
THE AUTHOR

Magnanimum patrem filia digna refert

PREFACE TO THIRD EDITION

———◆———

ON page 127, Mr. Gladstone is reported by me to have ascribed the Encumbered Estates Act to Peel. It was really passed by Lord John Russell. On page 128, he is represented as having attributed the Devon Commission to Lord Palmerston. The Commission was, in reality, appointed by Peel. How these mistakes arose it is hard to determine. With extreme diffidence I am inclined to attribute them to slips rather of attention than of memory on the part of my great (in a double sense) and lamented friend. It should be borne in mind that any colloquial inadvertence of his would have for its background and its excuse the pleasant and leisurely freedom—the *otium cum comitate*—of what was both literally and metaphorically a symposium.

The foregoing explanation appears to me plausible. On the other hand, I find it hard to imagine that the words addressed to me by Mr. Gladstone were completely forgotten, or rather misheard. It is worth noting that the two errors above mentioned occurred in a single conversation, a conversation which took place the last time that Mr. Gladstone ever dined with me. Extra precautions were taken on that occasion. At the dinner-table, in defiance of usage and for the convenience of hearing and being heard, the great man was sandwiched between Mrs. Tollemache and me; both she and I paid great attention to his remarks; and my report of them, which was drawn up at the earliest opportunity, was carefully revised by her.

I enter into these details because I am anxious to clear myself from the charge of what I would designate as the unpardonable sin in a Boswell; for, in very truth, the accuracy of a Boswell ought, like Cæsar's wife, to be above suspicion.

L. A. T.

NOTE

I HAVE received a letter from an intimate friend of Mr. Gladstone's, who spent a week with the great statesman shortly after he had left Biarritz for the last time, and who in the matter now before us is a highly competent authority. "His [Mr. Gladstone's] observations to you," he writes, "must have been due to some misunderstanding, probably caused by his deafness."

TALKS WITH MR. GLADSTONE

INTRODUCTION

Non te facundia, non te
Restituet pietas.

I saw something of Mr. Gladstone between 1856 and 1870 in England; and, after an interval of twenty years, I saw much of him at Biarritz. In reporting a few of the things that he said to me during the earlier period, I have to trust my memory entirely. His remarks during the later period have been carefully noted down. I am, therefore, confident that those remarks are reported with accuracy. Naturally, however, my attention was concentrated on Mr. Gladstone's observations; and I must add that the effort of committing those observations to memory, and likewise of replying to them, was such that I cannot pretend that my own part in the conversation is given with equal exactness. But this, of course, is a matter of minor importance. Another of my Boswellian canons ought, perhaps, to be disclosed. Several times my conversations with Mr. Gladstone were interrupted just when he was entering on an important subject; and I naturally endeavoured, during one or more subsequent interviews, to draw him out more thoroughly. When the drawing-out process had been completed and I had to make a final report of all that he had said, I had to choose between two alternatives, each of them open to objection. Sometimes I thought it safer to observe strict accuracy by referring the two or more mutually supplementing, not to say *overlapping*, conversations to the times when they respectively occurred. But more frequently I have consulted the convenience of my readers by following a logical, instead of a chronological arrangement, and by soldering together the disunited parts of what was practically a single dialogue.

In preparing to add to my literary gallery its most conspicuous portrait, I am confronted with the question: In order to concentrate attention on the portrait itself, ought not its frame to be as simple as possible? Or, to lay aside metaphor, ought I not to restrict myself to the mechanical office of Boswellizing Mr. Gladstone, and to leave the thankless task of criticising him to such biographers as are at once compelled and competent to discharge it? The question, when thus put, seems to answer itself; but the matter, in fact, is not so simple as at first sight appears. On the whole, the self-denying ordinance which I am inclined to impose on myself is this, that I should in general not presume to sit in judgment on Mr. Gladstone except in cases where my intercourse with him serves to throw light on some misunderstood parts of his character; or where, on the other hand, some remarks on his character are needed to throw light on my intercourse with him.

On neither of these two accounts do I feel called upon to say much about him as a statesman. Being forced to spend three-quarters of every year on the Continent in a sort of valetudinarian exile, I have come to regard myself, not certainly as an outlaw, but as what I may call an *outpolitics*,—as one who can look on party politics only from the standpoint of a philosophical outsider; so that, for this as well as for other reasons, I abstain from acting the part of a political censor. And this abstinence is, in the present case, made easier by the fact that the tie which bound him to me and mine was not political, but personal. He was a county neighbour of my Conservative father and of my more Conservative father-in-law (the late Lord Egerton of Tatton). When he and they were in the House of Commons together, he met them on a footing of friendly opposition; and although the political antagonism went on increasing, the friendly relations were perhaps not lessened down to the end of the chapter. The result of all this was that, when he extended his friendship to my wife and me, he showed a manifest disinclination to discuss the politics of the day. He seldom approached burning questions in my presence, and hardly ever in the presence of my wife. I could have wished that he had been less scrupulous ; but perhaps, after all, the loss was not very serious. The political Gladstone has long been, and will long continue to be, in everybody's mouth. It is of the non-political Gladstone that people in general need to learn something.

When I pass on from the public to the private character of Mr. Gladstone, I am only too sensible alike of the difficulty and of the necessity of touching on that most delicate part of my subject. To quote Cicero : " Quid dicam de moribus facillimis, de bonitate in suos, justitia in omnes ? " (*What should I say of the easy urbanity of his manners, of his goodness to his intimates, of his justice towards all men ?*) What, in particular, should I say, or forbear to say, about Mr. Gladstone's great kindness to me ? Compliments, however sincere and however well deserved, have nearly always an air of patronage; and, indeed, I have sometimes thought that the step from the sublime to the ridiculous is perhaps less short than the step from an ill-turned or ill-timed compliment to an insult. Those of us who are haunted by any such impression as is here indicated are naturally disposed, in relation to Mr. Gladstone's private virtues, to say less than we feel, or rather to keep silence even from good words. Nevertheless, it would be churlish in us to refrain altogether from bearing our eye-witnessing testimony to his considerate and *uncondescending* graciousness towards such of his juniors as he befriended. And we ourselves are led to do this all the more in order, so to say, to take away the unpleasing taste of the few

words of adverse criticism which will perforce make
their way into the following pages. Let it, then, be
understood once for all that, however we may have
differed from his views both on things present and
on things to come, we nevertheless judge him to
have exhibited an absolutely unique combination of
political sagacity with an unwavering conviction of
the Divine presence and support; so that we might
almost literally apostrophise him in the phrase of
the Greek poet—

" ἀνδρῶν σε πρῶτον ἔν τε ξυμφοραῖς βίου
κρίνοντες ἔν τε δαιμόνων ξυναλλαγαῖς."

I have mentioned that Mr. Gladstone, in his intercourse with me, seldom penetrated within the
recesses of politics. He, however, often led me into
what may be called the antechamber of politics. He
freely imparted to me his reminiscences; and those
reminiscences were interspersed with suggestive
comments, and had always, if I may so express it,
a *quorum pars magna fui* flavour about them.
When he was disposed to dwell on this interesting subject, I did my best to make him stick to
it; and, on other occasions, I threw the subject in
his path. His anecdotical reflections on such men
as Canning and Peel, as Lord Palmerston and
Disraeli, are reported with the utmost possible
minuteness.

There were, however, subjects on which he conversed with less interest and effect, and in reference
to which my duties as a reporter were less clear.
Of those less important remarks of his, should any,

or should all, be placed before my readers? An example will serve to show the nature of my perplexity. How much am I to record of my impressions of Mr. Gladstone's views on Homer's ethics and theology? My introduction to those views took place in an odd manner. In my Oxford days I heard a lady ask Jowett what he thought of Mr. Gladstone's then recently published book on Homer. "It's mere nonsense," was the brief answer. Without passing so summary a verdict on Mr. Gladstone's work, or presuming to speak on the subject as an expert, I am at least aware that, as Juvenal might have said, he made the Syrian Jordan flow into the Scamander: he Catholicised Hellenism and almost canonised Homer. Indeed, it was with reference to Mansel's Bampton Lectures and Mr. Gladstone's Homeric speculation that, some forty years ago, the future Bishop Jeune said to Bishop Wilberforce that he "had not expected to see the time when Atheism would be demonstrated from the pulpit of St. Mary's, and when the member for the University of Oxford would advocate the worship of the Pagan divinities" (*Safe Studies*, p. 247). He evidently held, as I also hold, that Mr. Gladstone was utterly at fault when he tried to discover a defaced or rudimentary Trinity amid the débris of the Hellenic Pantheon. And, for myself, I will further maintain that from Mr. Gladstone's initial error in this matter—from his invention, if I may so say, of an Athanasian Iliad—has arisen a false note in many of his utterances on Homer. How much, then, am I to report of such of those utterances as I heard ? To this question I reply that, if the intimacy with which he honoured me had been continued and continually renewed through many years, instead of being practically confined to a score or so of conversations, I should doubtless, in my report of his sayings about Homer, have used the pruning-knife pretty freely. But, as the case now stands, and as my readers will doubtless wish to see something even of the less interesting aspects of this eminently interesting character, I have thought it better to reduce the pruning process to a minimum. Nor will such an examination of his defective side be unprofitable. For, in very truth, the saying of Cato that "wise men learn more from fools than fools learn from wise men," may be supplemented with a corollary that *more is to be learnt from the follies of the wise than from the common sense of fools*. And to the case now before us such a corollary has a special application. For the Homeric hallucination, as I cannot but think it, of Mr. Gladstone was no mere excrescence or (so to say) *lusus sapientiæ*, but was correlated with the rest of his spiritual growth ; it was, in fact, not so much the vagary of a scholar as the sorry refuge of a theologian at bay. Let us see how this is to be explained. The Comparative Method or, let us rather say, the Evolutionary Principle, when applied to the competing religions of the world, tends to bring out what they have in common, to group them all under a single law, and, if I may so say, to lessen the extreme inequality of rank which has hitherto prevailed among them.   It is true that to Evolution, interpreted in this wide sense, Mr. Gladstone would have strongly objected.   But none the less is it probable that, without knowing it, he had a sprinkling from the impetuous and ubiquitous "stream of tendency."   He caught the evolutionary contagion.   He became so far a *philosophe malgré lui* that he more or less *levelled up* the chief religions, as the alternative to *levelling* them *down*. Something of the divine he had to recognise in all of them, lest haply he should be constrained to erase the divine from all of them.   Thus he gradually came to regard the greatest poets of Hellenism as more or less inspired, not merely in the colloquial and metaphorical, but in something like the theological sense of the word—inspired, one may say vaguely, not merely from Mount Helicon, but from Mount Zion.   So that he essayed to hear, and at last imagined that he really heard, the far-off echo of a revelation in Homer.

The general line that I have taken about the indirectly theological views of Mr. Gladstone may be extended to his directly theological views.   But between the two cases there is a difference.   Most of my readers will probably agree with me in not attaching much weight to his Homeric speculations. But many of them will attach far more weight than I should to his opinions on theology.   Therefore, what he said to me on the latter subject is reported almost entire.

In conclusion, I need hardly insist that I am entering into no sort of competition with any complete biography of Mr. Gladstone which may have been, or may hereafter be, brought out by one or more distinguished men who have known him intimately both in his public and private character. How, indeed, could I, handicapped as I am, adventure on such an unequal race?

> "Quid enim tremulis facere artubus hædi
> Consimile in cursu possint et fortis equi vis?"

Let me then say, or rather repeat, that my present function is to produce what may be called an *ethograph* of Mr. Gladstone—a photograph of his moral and social physiognomy, exactly as it presented itself to me. Nor can I doubt that, somewhat in the spirit of Cromwell, he would himself have wished that impartial justice should be done to that moral physiognomy, a physiognomy which, like his natural face, had its harsh and untoward aspects, but which was all the more truly venerable for its wrinkled and, at first sight, repellent grandeur. It is superfluous for me to add that I shall be more than satisfied if, in the bewildering chapter of accidents, it should be written that even this little book is to contribute its jot and tittle of evidence, at once trustworthy and favourable towards the final judgment which will be pronounced on him by posterity. *Habent sua fata libelli:* singular fates they have sometimes, and such as, when little is expected, are not always disappointing.   L. A. T.

NOTE

SINCE writing this, I have come across a saying of Tennyson about Mr. Gladstone's Homeric speculations, which confirms the view taken in the foregoing pages : " Very pleasant and very interesting he [Gladstone] was, even when he discoursed on Homer, where most people think him a little hobby-horsical : let him be. His hobby-horse is of the intellect and with a grace." This opinion should be compared or contrasted with the opinion entertained by Lake. In a letter of mine, entitled "Dr. Lake at Balliol," which was pub·lished in the *Spectator* (Jan. 1, 1898), there is a passage which I am tempted to quote, concluding as it does with a high and just compliment paid by the future Dean of Durham to Mr. Gladstone. It should be mentioned that the conversation referred to occurred in my undergraduate days, some forty years ago. "I once found Lake reading Mr. Gladstone's book on Homer, which had then been recently published, and I remarked to him that, in Jowett's opinion, the distinguished author had ascribed more to Homer than Homer himself ever dreamt of ; was this criticism just ? 'Possibly to some extent,' answered Lake, with a grim smile. 'But Mr. Jowett would allow only a *minimum*. I think there is more in Homer, just as I think there is more in the Bible, than he would acknowledge.' Then, with an evident allusion to my veneration for Jowett, he touched on the propensity of youth towards somewhat promiscuous hero-worship. His concluding words have stuck in my memory : ' In all my life I have only known three men of commanding great·ness—Arnold, Newman, Gladstone.' "

TALKS WITH MR. GLADSTONE

1856–1870

I

"Nec vero ille in luce modo atque in oculis civium magnus, sed intus domique præstantior."

CICERO.

"Seen him I have, but in his happier hour
Of social pleasure, ill-exchanged for power."

POPE.

IT was a proud moment for me when Mr. Gladstone, who was then canvassing the Oxford electors, called on me during my first year of residence at Balliol. Between 1856 and 1870 I saw him several times, chiefly in London and during two visits which I paid at Hawarden. But, instead of wearying my readers with the whereabouts and the *whenabouts* of my interviews with him, I will at once jot down some sayings of his which belong to this first period of our acquaintance.

My father, not realising to what extent I was handicapped by physical drawbacks, was continually urging me to go to the Bar. At his request, I laid the matter before Mr. Gladstone. Mr. Gladstone thought that my extreme nearsightedness would be an almost insuperable obstacle to my success at the Bar. I asked him if I should try diplomacy. His reply was not encouraging. Indeed, he said that he should not wish a son of his to become a diplomatist. He did not give his reasons; but I suspect that a thought was in his mind similar to that which prompted Macaulay to write: "Every calling has its peculiar temptations. There is no injustice in saying that diplomatists, as a class, have always been more distinguished by their address, by the art with which they win the confidence of those with whom they have to deal, and by the ease with which they catch the tone of every society into which they are admitted, than by generous enthusiasm or austere rectitude."

He went on to recommend to me a Parliamentary career; Parliamentary work would be less trying to the eyesight than practice at the Bar. He presently spoke of "official" life. Since he had been in office, he had learnt how much of the business could be deputed to trained subordinates; indeed, he had bestowed some pains on the art of thus working by proxy. Had I ever thought of trying to get into the House of Commons? I replied that I had turned Whig, to the no small perturbation of my kinsfolk. My father, who was then in the House of Commons, and who was a strong aristocrat and a still stronger autocrat, would never have tolerated my voting against him on any question which he deemed important. Mr. Gladstone seemed surprised, and added that public opinion appeared to him to be in an unhealthy state in regard to the nature and limits of the *patria potestas*. If a son of his own had differed from him in politics, he would have advised him not to enter public life till he was twenty-six; after that age, the son would be free to take an independent line. Mr. Gladstone thought it monstrous that Lord Stanley (the late Lord Derby), who was then about forty years old, should be practically compelled to join the Conservative party, in opposition to what were believed to be his private convictions. At the time of this conversation I myself was in my twenty-fifth year. Mr. Gladstone advised me to decide on a profession soon. After twenty-five the mind could not easily take a fresh direction, though it might make great progress in a direction already taken.

He did not, let me here repeat, often talk to me about politics; but I remember his once saying, with great emphasis, that the years which followed the close of the Great War seemed to him to be among the most disgraceful in our history: "The Tory Government passed a new Corn Law."

I asked him whether he did not think that the days of the English aristocracy were numbered. Might not what Tennyson says of religious systems be applied to aristocracies: "They have their day, and cease to be"? In other words, was not De Tocqueville right in thinking that, by an inexorable law, all things make for democracy? Mr. Gladstone answered that this broad statement of De Tocqueville appeared to him to be founded on a hasty generalisation. In particular, he thought that the feudal sentiment and traditions were deeply rooted in England.   He defended his opinion by citing two examples which, I own, did not appear to me very conclusive.   One of them I will repeat, as nearly as I can remember it.   He told me that a certain peer, who was a friend of his, had recently died.   He himself had consulted the man of business as to the choice of an agent who would give satisfaction to the tenants.   The man of business replied that what would please the tenants most would be the appointment of an agent who could claim kinship with the late lord.

In July 1864, I was so fortunate as to meet Mr. Mill at breakfast with Mr. Gladstone.[1]   The two eminent men talked about the probable effect of the war between Prussia and Denmark.   Mr. Gladstone mentioned that a high financial authority had expressed the opinion that, if Canada were ever annexed by the United States, the value of land in Canada would be greatly increased (I think he said " doubled "); and I understood Mr. Gladstone to add that, in like manner, the value of land in Schleswig-

---

[1] Some fragments of the remarks made by Mr. Mill on this, to me, memorable occasion, are indicated in *Safe Studies*, p. 263, and in the *Memoir of Jowett*, p. 101 (note).   I am tempted here to report another observation which Mr. Mill then made.   He told me that his father used to say that all war would speedily be brought to an end if only, in every battle, the soldiers on each side would direct all their efforts towards shooting the commander-in-chief of the opposite party.   I asked him whether, if this practice were set on foot, commanders-in-chief would not soon learn, like Ahab at Ramoth Gilead, to resort to the obvious expedient of a disguise.   " Yes," he replied gloomily, " I am afraid that the causes of war lie too deep for so simple a remedy."

Holstein would be increased by the annexation of those provinces to such an active and progressive nation as Prussia.

Mr. Gladstone went on to talk of his own somewhat romantic mission to Greece. He appeared to think that the old Greek type of countenance still lingered in Continental Greece more than is commonly supposed. I reminded him of the statement quoted by Gibbon from a Byzantine historian that "all Greece has been slavonised and become barbarous." "Yes," replied Mr. Gladstone, "I remember the passage well; and does not Gibbon go on to say that the language is as barbarous as the idea?" I have thought this worth recording as serving to show that, little as he sympathised with Gibbon, he yet knew Gibbon's *History* well.

He told Mr. Mill that he had never witnessed such complete and contented idleness as at Corfu. He related that he had there seen three men leisurely occupied in driving two turkeys along the road. Before pronouncing a judgment on this queer *otium sine dignitate*, one would wish to know what were its antecedent conditions, and how far the instance was a typical one.

I well remember a long walk which I took with Mr. Gladstone one Sunday afternoon at Hawarden. In the course of it, I referred to Mill's contention that slave-grown cotton was exhausting the soil of the Southern States, and that, even from a purely commercial point of view, emancipation was likely to be a gain; was Mr. Gladstone of the same opinion?

He replied that he abhorred slavery, but that he nevertheless feared that abolition would, in the first instance at any rate, be attended with financial difficulties.

I went on to ask him how he explained the strong antipathy expressed by nearly all Anglo-Americans for coloured men. The repulsion thus inspired by the typical negro is commonly described as physical and as irremediable, being, in fact, of the nature indicated by Sydney Smith in his famous adaptation of Virgil—

> "Et, si non alium late jactaret odorem,
> *Civis* erat."

Macaulay had said in conversation that, in his opinion, there was much exaggeration in this and kindred statements; he found it hard to reconcile them with the very close personal relation which not unfrequently subsists between individuals of the two races. Did not Mr. Gladstone also think that the antipathy in question is, in great part, born of imagination? His answer was decidedly in the affirmative. In support of his opinion, he mentioned the case (to which I shall have occasion to revert further on) of a negro gentleman whom he had himself known, and who was, not merely agreeable and accomplished, but distinguished by the refinement of his manners.

We fell to talking about physiognomy. He gave me the impression of more or less agreeing with Duncan, that there is no art to find the mind's construction in the face. In defence of his view, he cited the example of a distinguished politician who was then in the House of Commons, and who had been one of the pioneers of Free Trade: "I detest his countenance; but I believe that a more upright and honourable man never lived." There was something "intense" in Mr. Gladstone's voice as he said this, which was typical of his mode of conversing. His talk was not rhetorical; but it was emphatically the talk of an orator. In other words, it was not through rounded sentences, nor through a spouting, and, so to say, rounding delivery, but through the frequent use of strong phrases vocally italicised, and perhaps I should add, through the not infrequent accumulation of nearly synonymous epithets where perhaps a single epithet would have sufficed, that the note of the orator was discernible in his discourse.

It was, if my memory serves me, on the evening of the same Sunday that Mr. Gladstone conversed with me about the Classics and likewise about Theology. I asked some questions about the Homeric poems; and when I presently expressed a fear that I was boring him, he very graciously cut short my apology by saying that, after all the tumult and bustle of politics, he felt himself "in heaven" when he was breathing the pure atmosphere of Homer. He appeared to me, I confess, less to advantage when he passed into the region of Theology. I was so audacious as to make some strictures on the character of David. Were the vindictive and perfidious injunctions given by the dying king to his successor easily reconciled with his claim to be accounted a man after God's own heart? During this part of our conversation the late Lord Lyttelton was present, and made the very natural remark that this was an old *crux*, but that he thought the difficulty could be got over. What surprised me about Mr. Gladstone was that, in this part of the discussion, he seemed to be treading on new ground. Perhaps his mind was preoccupied, or I may have failed to understand him; but he certainly seemed to me to speak as if he was puzzled to make out what I meant, and as if this whole class of objections had never crossed his mind.

Our controversy on Old Testament ethics was merely an episode in a friendly discussion on one of Mr. Gladstone's favourite topics. He said that he had one fault to find with the Oxford Liberals which he could never get over: they made such small account of Bishop Butler. I did my best to clear up the anomaly which so embarrassed and pained him; but the solution which I offered did not satisfy him. As I shall have occasion to revert to this subject, it may obviate the necessity of further explanation if I state, more explicitly than I ventured to state to Mr. Gladstone, the causes which excite in some Oxford Liberals so strong an antipathy to what he called the " Butlerian " system. It must be premised that many of those Liberals regard Butler as a less logical Mansel; insomuch that Mansel's Bampton Lectures may be described as Butler's *Analogy* writ plain. Now, Oxford

Liberals of the class indicated by Mr. Gladstone generally sympathise with what may be termed the Left Centre of Theology, and perhaps, next to that, with the Right Centre. On the other hand, Butler's and Mansel's reasoning is a weapon which the Extreme Right and the Extreme Left combine to use against the Right Centre and the Left Centre, but which they are powerless to employ against one another. Nay, we may go the length of saying that the weapon which Catholics employ with such deadly effect against the orthodox Protestant is the self-same Butlerian weapon wherewith he himself is wont, so confidently and so pitilessly, to transfix all Liberal Protestants—

> "The treacherous instrument is in thy hand,
> Unbated and envenomed."

Nor is this all. The argument of the *Analogy*, if pressed to its conclusions, would interdict the application of our human standard of ethics to any alleged divine revelation, and would consequently yield everything to the faith which, if the phrase may be allowed, bids highest in miracles. I once heard Jowett make the admission that, on that principle, a strong case might be made out for Brahminism. At all events, without presuming to award the thaumaturgical palm, his disciples are dismayed when they reflect with what ease and with what fatal results the too accommodating and transferable, or, as Bunyan might have said, *facing both ways*, logic of Butler could be turned to account by the enemies of religion. For, as viewed from the standpoint of those enemies, the argument of Butler and Mansel amounts to this, " If we are not prepared to believe everything, we must believe nothing. *Gardez-vous de ce premier pas qui coûte.* Give Supernaturalism an inch, and it claims the Universe."

And now, before proceeding to my later and longer conversations with Mr. Gladstone, I propose to make one or two of those illustrative comments of which I have already spoken. With this object in view, it will be convenient to go back a little. When preparing myself for my first visit to Hawarden, I had a talk with an able man whose name I will not disclose, but of whom I will say that he knew Mr. Gladstone well ; and I asked him (in effect) so to furbish me up intellectually that I might not be wholly unpresentable when brought face to face with the great man. Especially did I wish to know whether it would be safe to express modern views in his presence. What has already been related may be taken as in some sort answering this question. Nevertheless, it may be of use to report the answer, or rather the general account of Mr. Gladstone, which my experienced informant gave me. He advised me to beware, during my stay at Hawarden, of expressing heretical opinions before my orthodox host. Mr. Gladstone, he went on to say, was distinguished by two great qualities, each of which he possessed in an extraordinary degree, and the combination of which he possessed in a degree almost, if not quite, unprecedented.

These qualities were, first, the oratorical faculty, and, secondly, the power of mastering details. But the oratorical faculty has its drawbacks. Being so strongly developed in Mr. Gladstone, it generated in him an abnormal, if not morbid, intensity of purpose. Whatsoever his mind or his head found to do, he did it with his might. The result was that his intellect grew to be like the giant oak, wanting in pliancy by reason of its massive strength. His difficulty in sympathising with opponents was measured by his unfaltering conviction — a conviction as intense as that of St. Paul or of Savonarola—that his own cause was the cause of God. My friend concluded by telling me that the great orator's eager and, as it were, hypnotic absorption in whatever he took up was sometimes apparent even in trivial matters, and that at such times it was apt to become extravagant, and even oppressive : " He will talk about a piece of old china as if he was standing before the judgment-seat of God."

" I have," said Charles Lamb, " an almost feminine partiality for old china." Probably this predilection was the only point which Lamb and Mr. Gladstone had in common. And, even in that point of resemblance, there was a marked difference between the two men. For, in the case of Mr. Gladstone, this " feminine partiality," as it were, put on virility through its contact with his eminently masculine nature. How quixotic, or rather how Quixote-like, how grandly fantastic he was in that infatuation, even as in his infatuation about Helen of Troy ! I never ceased to be grateful to the late Lady de Tabley who, one evening when she and I were guests of the Gladstones, espied me *nescio quid meditantem nugarum* in a distant corner, and hurried me across the room just in time to see Mr. Gladstone holding up a piece of old china, and to take note of the flashing eye and the Rhadamanthine solemnity with which the great enthusiast was winding up his discourse.

Passing on to a less quaintly trivial matter, I will add another example of the way in which Mr. Gladstone, in what may be termed his intellectual paintings, was apt to lay on the colours too thick. A distinguished Liberal told me, many years ago, that he had asked Mr. Gladstone if he did not think it a matter of regret that the young men of the time seemed to take little interest in the debates in the House of Commons. Mr. Gladstone laid his hand on my friend's arm, and explained with awe-inspiring emphasis that the indifference thus shown by the rising generation appeared to him to be a "plague-spot" in the body politic. My informant, though himself a very earnest man, evidently thought that Mr. Gladstone, by his vehement and, so to say, Apocalyptic use of language, showed a certain want of moral perspective.

It will now be understood what Walter Bagehot meant by saying of him :—

"He is interested in everything he has to do with, and often interested too much. He proposes to put a stamp on contract notes with an eager earnestness as if the destiny of Europe here and hereafter depended upon its enactment. . . . The oratorical impulse is a *disorganising* impulse. The higher faculties of the mind require a certain calm, and the excitement of oratory is unfavourable to that calm."

The latter part of this extract may seem irrelevant; but I quote it as leading up to a matter on which I wish to touch briefly. I had a talk with Jowett about Mr. Gladstone some forty years ago, that is to say, before he had begun to entertain the antipathy for him which he freely expressed in later years. What, I asked, did he make of the fact that this most religious of our politicians was often charged with being dishonest? His answer was on this wise: "Gladstone is not dishonest; but it is natural that persons who do not understand him should think him dishonest." He went on to make some explanatory and other general remarks; but the only one of those remarks that I can distinctly recall is, that he expressed a better opinion of Mr. Gladstone than of Bishop Wilberforce. His explanation, however, left certain vague impressions on my mind; and I have often felt a wish, as an architect might say, to *restore* that explanation, or rather to give shape to the general impression which I myself have derived from this and from more direct sources. How came it about, let me repeat, that this conspicuously upright and conscientious statesman was so grievously misunderstood? Such a misunderstanding, if not accounted for as founded on some plausible error, is thought to warrant the suspicion of being founded on fact; and therefore, without pretending wholly to clear up the misconstruction under which Mr. Gladstone laboured, I feel bound, after enjoying the privilege of his friendship, to throw out one or two explanatory suggestions.

Let me, then, begin by observing that the faults of a great and good man always stand out conspicuously in relief. Not only are they conspicuous because he is conspicuous, and because they are seen in broad contrast to his virtues, but also because the high ideal which he sets up is a standing rebuke to the self-complacent mediocrity of his neighbours, and tempts them to indemnify themselves by means of reprisals; insomuch that to the saint or hero as well as to the Pharisee—to him who, holding high and, as it were, reproachful ideals, strives to act up to them, as well as to him who does not—should the Divine caution be addressed: " With what measure ye mete it shall be measured to you again." Mr. Gladstone, in particular, stood in need of this caution. Being an orator, he was wont to think and to speak with his emotions at red heat, and to give utterance to burning and provocative words when he passed censure on folly and sin. Also, he laid himself open to attack by his political change of front. No doubt this transition of his, in an age of transition, was in a sense appropriate, and furnished one of the many proofs of his conscientiousness. " To live is to change," says Newman, " and to be perfect is to have changed often." There is some truth in this observation, though it is too broadly expressed, and though it comes oddly from an upholder of the most unbending of creeds. But, at any rate, to rank changefulness of this kind as a virtue is to set up a *counsel of imperfection*. "Unstable as water," says the Scripture, "thou shalt not excel"; and assuredly the man of many changes, the sort of man whom Aristotle would have called a chameleon, cannot hope to inspire confidence. He is liable to excite an apprehension that (if I may so express myself) he may one day become a *re-turncoat*, or else may be, not a turncoat only, but a *turn waistcoat* as well; in other words, he may either go back, or else go forward too fast and too far. Thus it was that, being at once an orator and (in the literal sense) a renegade, Mr. Gladstone was severely handled, and ran the risk of being overwhelmed by a flood of invectives. In fear of such submersion, he caught at straws, and persuaded himself that they were solid planks. To lay aside metaphor, he was subtle and even sophistical in his explanations of his devious courses. Yet in giving these explanations he was perfectly sincere.

Sincerity under these conditions would have been impossible to a philosopher; but it came easily to such a typical orator as Mr. Gladstone. For the typical orator, in whom, as in women, feeling is believing, resembles women likewise in their perilously convenient capacity for self-deception. But the hallucinations of the orator, those veritable *eidola fori*, are just what Philistines cannot, and political opponents will not, understand. Nor can

3

it be denied that on that ground the opponents of Mr. Gladstone could build up a plausible case. Thus, when Disraeli said of him that "he was inebriated with the exuberance of his own verbosity," it must be admitted that in that eminently Disraelitish phrase—itself not conspicuous for the simplicity of its diction—there was the element of truth that Mr. Gladstone was sometimes not the master but the servant of his emotions, and even of his metaphors. The result of all this was that, in the popular imagination, his subtlety of reasoning came to be associated with that moral indirectness which the word subtlety often connotes. Indeed, his unconscious special pleading was at last mistaken for deliberate insincerity. Hence it appears that the dishonesty of which he has often been accused, resolves itself into the seeming dishonesty of an orator who is also a man of action, or (let us say) of a statesman who often unwittingly has recourse to compromises such as he has often eloquently denounced; it is, in fact, *dishonesty simulated by impassioned honesty.* For, in very truth, a saintly enthusiast, seeking to practise all that he has preached, is trying to maintain himself on a level too high for human nature (*ceratis ope Daedalea Nititur pennis*).[1]

[1] The difficulty of keeping aloft, during a long period, at the enthusiastically moral, or rather at the apostolic, level is set forth by Renan forcibly, though doubtless with some exaggeration. Referring to the protracted and checquered career of Mahomet, and apparently making at the same time an indirect allusion to the early death of One greater than Mahomet, he observes: "L'homme

With this *intensity*, born of oratorical sensibility, was closely connected another aspect of Mr. Gladstone's mind, which must be mentioned as throwing light on certain parts of his conversations with me. He was not affected or afflicted with that need of laughing to prevent weeping, with that mingled sense of world-humour and of world-pathos—in short, with that appetite for the incongruous — which is a characteristic product of decadence, and which, like a fair plant springing up from a manured soil, derives much of its sustenance from the noisome tragedies of life. Indeed, he had no toleration—I had almost said no comprehension—of that Epicurean and, so to say, Renanesque quality which French writers call "ironie" and Bagehot has called "pleasant cynicism." Perhaps I should be merely expressing the same thought in other words if I were to say that, himself demanding much from human nature, he had no sympathy or patience with those who demanded little from it. In short, he would not, like Pope, have declared the "ninth beatitude" to be "Blessed is he who expects nothing, for he shall never be disappointed." Rather would he have agreed with Kingsley in calling that a "devil's beatitude." It is not necessary to dwell further on this side of Mr. Gladstone's character. Suffice it to say that his rooted aversion to cynicism and scepticism of all sorts may serve to explain the tone

est trop faible pour porter longtemps la mission divine, et ceux-là seuls sont immaculés que Dieu a bientôt déchargés du fardeau de l'apostolat.'

of some of his observations recorded in the sequel. Especially may it account for the severity with which he spoke to me of Talleyrand, and even of Matthew Arnold, and for his earnest exhortation to keep alive the sense of sin.

Dean Swift, hearing someone described as "a fine old man," petulantly exclaimed: "A fine old man? There is no such thing. If the man you speak of had either a mind or a body worth a farthing, they would have worn him out long ago." Could such an inhuman outcry of despair have proceeded from anyone who had known our wise orator and statesman when the mellowing hand of time had passed upon him, and who had felt, when the news came that he too had gone to his rest in the eternal, how sad was the loss, not to his friends only, but to his country?

Personally, I have often thought that the noble, if somewhat invidious, tribute of praise which was originally bestowed on Tiresias, and which Cato applied to the younger Scipio, could be transferred to the veteran Gladstone—

"'Οἴῳ πεπνῦσθαι, τοὶ δὲ σκιαὶ ἀΐσσουσιν." [1]

For truly in this estimable but mediocre generation of ours—this generation so prolific of talent, but so barren of genius—he stood forth, during the closing

[1] Translated in North's *Plutarch*—
　　"This only man right wise reputed is to be;
　　All other seem but shadows set, by such wise men as he."

years of his life, as a monumental relic of a mightier age which has passed away. To those closing years I now transport my readers. Our scene is transferred from England to Biarritz, at the same time that our drama (after the manner of the *Winter's Tale*) overleaps a score of years. Let me add that henceforward the report of the dialogues will be in a quasi-dramatic, or, to speak more exactly, in a Boswellian and diaristic form.

TALKS WITH MR. GLADSTONE

1891–1896

II

"Sideris instar
Emicuit Stilichonis apex, et cognita fulsit
Canities."

CLAUDIAN.

(*Paraphrased*)
"A Grand Old Man."

HÔTEL D'ANGLETERRE, BIARRITZ.

December 1891.—Mr. Gladstone called on us. He complained that Butler is not cared for on the Continent. Kant had been influenced by him, and acknowledged it; Lotze also spoke in high terms of him. Mr. Gladstone was slow in seeing what I meant when I said that the argument of Butler's *Analogy* is many-sided: that, if it disables human reason from dealing with the moral anomalies of one religion, it gives the like negative support to all religions; and that, in fact, it may as easily be used in defence of the massacre of St. Bartholomew, and even of Thuggee, as in defence of Joshua's massacres and Jael's treachery. He said that he did not remember that Butler referred to these, but afterwards admitted that his argument might be so applied. I said that Catholics might think that

41

Butler's argument told more for them than for us. He hardly seemed to see my point, but said that Catholicism seemed to be the only subject on which Butler lost his usual impartiality and became violent. He said that Lotze and others valued Butler mainly as a theologian; he himself valued him even more as a philosopher; he called him "*the* guide through the perplexities of thought and conduct in modern life." On the side of the importance of Butler, unwilling testimony, he said, was given by Mark Pattison: "The pains that he took to dethrone my idol are significant." He also quoted Miss Hennell, who wrote a pamphlet called *On the Sceptical Tendencies of Butler's "Analogy."* He thought that this pamphlet had not received the attention it deserved. Miss Hennell, while attacking Butler, expresses her strong admiration for him. He thought that the neglect of Butler was a blot upon Oxford.

He said that his only complaint against Biarritz was that the society was too exclusively English. On my saying that I chiefly complained of its want of intellectuality, he went off on the subject of the great intellectual progress made by women. He had written an article in the *Speaker* on the great number of poetesses who were scarcely known as they deserved to be. He spoke of Mrs. Browning as the only exception. I referred to George Eliot; but he would not admit her claim. He mentioned Miss Constance Naden, Emily Brontë, Lady Charlotte Eliot, and Mrs. Clive, the authoress of " X Poems by V." He referred especially to her poem on "Invitations to the Queen's Ball," as dealing with an unpromising subject, but showing powerful imagination. He had talked on the subject of these overlooked poetesses with Tennyson, who agreed with him.

Referring to Charles Austin, he spoke with disappointment of his having done so little in after life. I asked whether he did not think that men, not very strong physically, sometimes overstrained themselves when young, and that then, like the flowering aloe, they were completely exhausted. He admitted this, and added that a career like that of Charles Austin was especially open to objection, as withdrawing very able men from leaving anything of permanent value.[1] I asked whether he was referring to the Bar in general or to the Parliamentary Bar in particular. He replied that he meant the latter, and instanced Hope Scott.

I accompanied him to the Grand Hôtel, where he was staying. He characteristically remarked that this hotel has seven gates, and that he called it ἑπτάπυλοι Θῆβαι.

December 23, 1891.—I dined with Mr. Armitstead and the Gladstones. Mr. Gladstone said that

---

[1] When commenting on my *Recollections of Charles Austin*, Fitzjames Stephen applied to Austin's ineffectual life the lament of Carlyle : "Oh, the Bar, the Bar ! I look on it as just a great devouring gulf that eats up all the sturdy fellows that might help us in our sorrows."

the science of "pre-history" is quite new; and he went on to remark that the Basques pay greater respect to women now than anyone in Europe paid to them in the Middle Ages.

He spoke of the English literature of the nineteenth century as "quite extraordinary." He thought this strange, "because of the Elizabethan outburst." He said that there had been practically continuity, and that this was very rare, and was, moreover, a great disadvantage to living poets. No book nowadays produces an excitement at all equal to that caused by Walter Scott's novels. The nearest approach was the interest shown in Tennyson's last poems; but this was not at all equal to the interest awakened by Scott.

A young lady present sprung a mine by saying that Scott was dull, and adding that she got more pleasure from Thackeray and George Eliot. She was more flattered than provoked by the half angry earnestness with which Mr. Gladstone said, "We shall never agree about novels." The young lady then said that she would recognise Maggie Tulliver if she spoke to her, but that she would not recognise one of Scott's heroines. Scott's queens seemed to her, like a child's notions of a queen, and to have nothing distinctive. "What, does he make no difference between Queen Mary and Queen Elizabeth?" he asked indignantly. She inquired what modern novels he admired. He replied by calling Mr. Baring Gould's *Mehalah* a very powerful novel; but he seemed to think that

novels are now too much the rage. He spoke of
the late Lord de Tabley as having written good
poetry which is not read, and bad novels which *are*
read.

We went on to discuss the general question of
how far Scott's heroes and heroines are lifelike.
It seemed to me that this question could be illustrated by referring to the more extreme case of
epic and tragic heroes. For example, the Homeric
Æneas, after challenging Achilles, inflicted on him
a somewhat irrelevant versified discourse; and
(stranger still) the great Achilles, although in a
hurry to kill as many Trojans as possible, listened
patiently to his enemy's tedious harangue, instead
of vanquishing him at once. So, likewise, Shakespeare represents Prince Arthur, after taking his
fatal leap from the Tower, as breathing out his soul
in a rhyming couplet. In view of such instances of
untimely versification, one was tempted jocularly
to say that the heroes of poetry combined the
eccentricities of mosquitoes and of swans: *they
sing before they molest, and they sing before they
die!* Seriously, if those inopportunely poetical
heroes are called natural and lifelike, what
poetical heroes can be called unnatural? Do not
these considerations apply literally to the heroes
of Scott's poems? and do not similar considerations
apply, though of course in a far less degree, to the
somewhat rhetorical and *tall-talking* heroes and
heroines of Scott's novels?

Mr. Gladstone's reply was, in effect, that Scott's

writings are in "the grand style." He compared them to the paintings of Raphael and of the Old Masters generally; and he went on to say that the pictures of the Royal Academy recall more exactly the men and women in modern novels and life. He added that you have no right to like a book better because you are in sympathy with it; on that principle, you would prefer the Royal Academy to the National Gallery. He might have gone a step further. "I know nothing of painting, and detest it," writes Byron, "unless it reminds me of something I have seen or think it possible to see." Probably the great majority of the persons who saunter through picture galleries would, if they had Byron's candour, avow that they share his sentiments. These formalists and art-pretenders, while they feel bound (as the phrase is) to "do" the National Gallery, really derive more pleasure from the Royal Academy; and, *mutatis mutandis*, they correspond to the startlingly large class of readers who prefer novels descriptive of common life to the novels of Scott.

Mr. Gladstone was evidently not well up in Browning; but he said that it was plain that Browning must be a remarkable man: he had got hold of the reading public; the existence of Browning Societies showed how much trouble people would take to learn the "grammar" of his language. Passing on to Mr. George Meredith, he said that one of his daughters had made him begin *Diana of the Crossways*; but he evidently stuck in it.

He thought that Scott was the greatest delineator of human character next to Homer and Shakespeare. He remarked that in Italy there had been a revival of poetry in Leopardi and others.

He maintained that there was a want of "harmony" in George Eliot's novels: "she makes such absurd people marry one another. Why did Adam Bede marry Dinah?" Is it, one cannot but ask, an objection to a novel that it makes the wrong people marry? If it is, does not the objection apply as much to *Kenilworth* or *The Bride of Lammermoor* as to *Adam Bede*? Surely in all such cases the novelist is simply realistic. He is seeking to embody in fiction the Horatian sentiment which is only too often justified by experience—

> "Sic visum Veneri, cui placet impares
> Formas atque animos sub juga aënea
> Sævo mittere cum joco."[1]

After talking of American novelists and contrasting them with Scott, Mr. Gladstone said that an American had declared that he did not suppose that there were ten men in Boston equal to Shakespeare. This reminds me that I was once assured by an old Indian judge that he had himself heard a Baboo student ingenuously declare that he had been reading Shakespeare and Milton, and hoped soon to produce a poem which would combine the merits of both!

Mr. Gladstone went on to mention some curious

---

[1] "Thus it hath seemed good to Venus, who loveth with cruel jest unequally to yoke together forms and minds unmeet."

"survivals." In Yorkshire are two places, Boston and Appleton, called by people on the other side of a ridge Bosby and Appleby. In the same neighbourhood the same family was called indiscriminately "—ton" and "—by." He regarded this as a survival of an old state of things. He spoke of an odd tenure in land in the Highlands, the land not being held in common, but divided periodically, he thought annually.

Referring to a report in the newspapers that the Comte de Paris acquiesced in the Republic, he said he was glad of it. A few years ago especially, when there were so many claimants to the French throne, the conduct of those claimants was "not mischievous merely, but ridiculous." He thought that the Franco-German War was almost entirely the act of the Emperor. The heads of departments had been asked about the general feeling in their own districts, and had in almost each instance answered that it was unfavourable to war; and even in the exceptional instances the feeling for war was described as lukewarm. One of the guests rejoined that he himself had been in Paris when the war was declared, and that then the feeling for it seemed to be very strong. Mr. Gladstone replied that Paris no doubt was more warlike than the provinces, but that it was very easy for the Government to excite a seeming enthusiasm. He referred to a caricature which appeared at the time, and which represented the words " Fermé jusqu' à la prise de Berlin " as written over the shop of a cobbler

who had opposed the war. I asked about *plébiscites.*
He replied: "The *plébiscite* was a mere imposture,
an enemy to liberty. No alternative to the Empire
was proposed; so that those who voted for the
Empire were choosing between it and anarchy."

I asked about the unpopularity of the Emperor
Frederick and the Empress. He said that she tried
too ostentatiously to Anglicise Germany; and that
Frederick, during his three months, had not time
to accustom the Germans to a complete change of
policy. Mr. Gladstone knew from experience how
little can be done in three months. He added that
the Germans have had no history of their own for
a long time, and this makes them extra-sensitive
about foreign innovations. Might not this argument
of his be turned the other way? Would not a
nation with a satisfactory history have at least as
good a cause to complain of imported institutions?

I spoke of the unexpectedly friendly attitude
which had recently been adopted by the young
Emperor towards England. Mr. Gladstone seemed
not over confident about this. I asked about the
fall of Bismarck.

Gladstone.—" According to English notions, Bismarck was clearly wrong; he insisted on his subordinates not communicating with the Emperor,
except through him."

Tollemache.—" Would it make much difference in
England if this were done?"

G.—" Immense; but I find it difficult to give the
reason. The working of the English Cabinet can

4

hardly be understood *ab extra*. It grew by degrees, and its history is unrecorded. The best account of it is in Morley's monograph on Sir Robert Walpole."

He explained that he did not mean that the subordinate Ministers could appeal to the Crown against the Prime Minister. If they differed from him, of course they would have to resign; but, in the ordinary discharge of their official duties, they could not be expected to submit all despatches to him. He said that in the *Life of the Prince Consort* a great exception is recorded. He thought that this occurred in 1851. Lord John Russell, then Prime Minister, insisted on seeing Lord Palmerston's despatches. Mr. Gladstone regretted that he had never cross-questioned Lord John about this. Lord John was well up in constitutional law and custom; and Mr. Gladstone supposed that he meant his conduct to be regarded as entirely exceptional and *pro re nata*. I asked him what he thought of Lord Palmerston as a speaker.

G.—" He had a happy faculty of making his words exactly fit his meaning. This does not sound a very uncommon thing; but it really is so. People are so apt to say more than they mean. Parnell is another striking instance of the same guardedness of expression."

T.—" My father was much struck by the speaking of Mr. Lowe."

G.—" In 1866 Lowe was quite at the top of the tree."

January 2, 1892.—Mr. and Mrs. Gladstone dined with us.

I said the old grace, *Benedictus benedicat*, and added that Charles Austin used always to say it. Mr. Gladstone remarked that it was adopted in the Nonconformist College at Oxford. He expressed great satisfaction at there being such a College, or rather two such; and he wished there was a Roman Catholic one. He said that Newman and the more liberal Catholics wished for one.

He regarded the reputed Editor of the *Spectator* (Mr Hutton) as being, at least since Matthew Arnold's death, the first of our critics. Since his own policy had been each week attacked in the *Spectator*, he had left off taking it in. He said that this was due to his great regard for the Editor: "I found that reading those weekly attacks tended, to use a vulgar term, to establish a raw."

I told the story that Matthew Arnold, when asked what he thought of *Robert Elsmere*, replied, "No Arnold could ever write a novel. Otherwise *I* should have written one!"

G.—"I have been told that Arnold did not consider that *Robert Elsmere* went far enough."

T.—"Arnold's theology, I should say, was more negative than Robert Elsmere's. But he clung to the Church as the symbol of his spiritual life; he was less of a Theist, but more of a Christian. He was a Neo-Christian, or rather a Neo-Anglican."

G.—"I understand that Matthew Arnold considered himself so far an Anglican as to take part in the discussions in Sion College."

T.—"I know that he used to take the Sacrament."

Being asked what he thought of Lord Rosebery's *Life of Pitt,* he said that he agreed with the first part of that work, but not with the second. He considered himself a Pittite in regard to the first part of Pitt's career, but a Foxite in regard to the second part.

I expressed some surprise at Lord Holland's having protested against Napoleon's being sent to St. Helena.

G.—"I believe that Napoleon narrowly escaped being shot, and I understand that Wellington was in favour of his execution. But I am glad that his life was spared."

T.—"I believe that this was also the wish of Blücher. How was it that, if the two generals were thus agreed, Napoleon escaped?"

G.—"The Emperor of Austria was naturally opposed to the execution of his own son-in-law; and I believe that, in spite of all that Russia had suffered, the Czar was of the same mind."

T.—"Charles Austin would not have minded if Napoleon had been shot after Waterloo. The bloodshed after the return from Elba was more due to Napoleon than to Ney or Labédoyère."

G.—"I am not defending the execution of Ney. At the same time, I think that much might have been urged in favour of Austin's view. But the evils of the French Revolution, and even of the First Empire,

should in great part be laid to the account of Louis
XIV. and XV., and even of Richelieu. These destroyed the sense of duty and of public spirit among
Frenchmen. The Terrorists were merely the funguses
which sprang up in the corrupt soil."

In regard to this reasoning I am tempted to object
that, if it may be pleaded in excuse for Robes-
pierre and Napoleon that their misdemeanours were
in some sort the outcome of previous conditions, may
not the same plea be urged on behalf of Richelieu
and the Bourbons? In fact, the shield of Philosophical Necessity should be cast over every one, or
over no one. Especially should we bear in mind
that the tyrannical acts of rulers bear some sort of
relation to the passivity of the masses. The guilt
of Phalaris, when he roasted shipwrecked mariners
alive in his sonorous bull, was to some degree shared
by his subjects, who tolerated, if they did not enjoy,
the pastime of the ὕμνος ἄυμνος, of the hideous
melody of murder. A less extreme example of the
solidarity that subsists between rulers and ruled is
well indicated by Cassius in *Julius Cæsar*—

> "And why should Cæsar be a tyrant then?
> Poor man! I know he would not be a wolf,
> But that he sees the Romans are but sheep:
> He were no lion, were not the Romans hinds."

G.—"Napoleon at St. Helena used to protest
against being compared with Cromwell; he used to
say that he had not cut off his king's head, but had
merely appeared as the Saviour of Society. Well, it
was the Allied Powers, and especially the English,

who, by making war on the French, frustrated every attempt of the Republic to set up a durable Government. And in the meantime the English labourer was impoverished. In 1812 he was ten times worse off than he now is. He received only half his present wages, and he had to pay five times as much for bread. At one time corn rose to 21s. a bushel; while now, or at least during the past few years, and until quite lately, he had only to pay 4s. a bushel."

Mr. Gladstone urged me to read the *Memoirs of Marbot*, who had unusual opportunities of seeing Napoleon at close quarters. He admitted, indeed, that Marbot sometimes drew the long-bow, as when he described himself as more than a match for three Englishmen. I compared this with the complete victory won by three Frenchmen over three English men in *Les trois Mousquetaires*. Mr. Gladstone more appropriately contrasted it with the assertion in *Henry V.*, that one Englishman is a match for three Frenchmen. Charles Kean had told him that, before Magenta and Solferino, the gallery always clapped this passage. After those French victories the clapping ceased. Mr. Gladstone quoted this as speaking well for the good sense and fairness of the English people.

Is there anything to be urged on the opposite side of the question? At any rate, I am tempted to supplement Mr. Gladstone's view by quoting, for what it is worth, an extract from one of Chesterfield's *Letters*: "That silly, sanguine notion, which is firmly entertained here, that one Englishman can beat three Frenchmen, encourages, and has sometimes enabled, one Englishman in reality to beat two."

The conversation passed on to English politics and lawyers.

T.—"My uncle, Lord Mount Temple, used to tell me that lawyers generally fail in Parliament. Was not Cockburn an exception?"

G.—"Cockburn's reputation in Parliament was founded on a single speech, in defence of Lord Palmerston. Take the case of another great lawyer. Sir George Jessel discussed legal questions with beautiful clearness, but became a mere partizan when discussing politics."

T.—"Lord Lansdowne once told Charles Austin that he thought Bright, as an orator, fully equal to Charles Fox." This seemed to surprise Mr. Gladstone. I referred to Sheridan's "Begum Speech" as having been ill reported.

G.—"The speeches in Parliament are ill reported even now. Questions asked before debate are accurately given; but, as for the rest, I can only apply to the reports what Kingsley said to the friend who consulted him about his poems, 'They are not good, but bad.' This is creditable to the reporters as men." He apparently meant that the reporters thus show that they take a human interest in what they hear and write.

G.—"The very same reporters would do their work much better in the country. It takes me twice as long to correct a speech in Parliament as to correct one of equal length in the country." He even complained of the inaccuracy of the reports of speeches in the *Times*; but other M.P.'s have spoken to me far more favourably of these reports in the *Times*. They think that Mr. Gladstone's difficulty in getting his speeches well reported, arose from the fact that at this time of his life he had, except when strongly excited, lost somewhat of his clear articulation.

G.—"Canning's speeches, as published in their collected form, are very different from what they were as originally reported."

I asked him if he had heard Canning's famous speech which was delivered in 1826, when the independence of the Spanish Colonies in the West was acknowledged by Great Britain, and which contained the exultant phrase, "I called the New World into existence to redress the balance of the Old."

G.—"No. I did not hear that speech but I heard two earlier ones. One was at Liverpool in 1822. It was called the 'Red Lion' speech. In this speech Canning satirised those who made reform a panacea, by comparing them to the painter who could paint nothing but red lions. In boudoirs small red lions were painted, in drawing-rooms bigger ones. Personally, I feel some sympathy with the people thus satirised. Another speech of Canning which I heard, contained a prediction of the future greatness of Lord John Russell; it was (in effect): 'I doubt not that the noble lord will become great, and that his principles will triumph; but, for myself, I am proud to be on the losing side.'"

I quoted *Victrix causa deis placuit, sed victa Catoni,* and might more appropriately have quoted the exclamation of Brutus after the battle of Philippi—

> "I shall have glory by this losing day,
> More than Octavius and Mark Antony
> By this vile conquest shall attain unto." [1]

Mr. Gladstone spoke of Bethell and Newman as the two most subtle masters of English prose of our time. He said that, in the affair of Sir John Bowring, the Government consulted its law officers as to Sir John's conduct towards China. Wortley, the Solicitor-General, seemed to think the case doubtful; but Bethell declared that Sir John had not a leg to stand upon. Afterwards he was called upon in Parliament to defend the Government, and so acute an observer as Sir Erskine May expressed an opinion that he had made out a strong case.

I remarked that the view taken of Lord Lyndhurst by Miss Martineau and Walter Bagehot was anything but flattering; and I mentioned the incident which was afterwards recorded in my article called "Lord Tollemache and his Anecdotes." "Charles

---

[1] I am sorry that I did not repeat, in this relation, the lines from Addison's *Cato*, which Mr. Gladstone's hero, Sir Walter Scott, when taking up ineffectual arms against a sea of troubles, manfully applied to himself—

> "'Tis not in mortals to command success,
> But we'll do more, Sempronius, we'll deserve it."

Austin related a fact illustrative of the bitter indignation which prevailed among the Whigs when Copley, like another Strafford, suddenly 'ratted' and turned Tory. So extreme was this resentment that Denman told his servant that, if his old friend called, he was not to be admitted. In spite of the servant, the future Lord Lyndhurst made his way to the door of Denman's chambers, and shouted from outside, 'Let me at least beg that, if you are asked about my change of opinions, you will say that it was honest.' 'If I am asked about your change of opinions,' was the reply from within, 'I will say that *you say* it was honest.'"[1]

Mr. Gladstone cautiously replied that Lord Lyndhurst was something of a statesman, and that he understood that his legal decisions carried weight.

T.—"My father told me that he had heard Peel speak with high praise of what he termed Cobden's 'unadorned eloquence.'[2] I only once heard Cobden speak, and he seemed to me then to be very wanting in fluency; he could not hit upon the right word. But this was shortly before he died; and my father afterwards told me that he had never before known him to be so unsuccessful."

G.—"I never knew Cobden pause for a word; it

[1] *Fortnightly Review*, July 1892, p. 74.

[2] The classical reader will be reminded of the praise bestowed by Cicero on Cæsar's eloquence, which he describes as bare of all ornament, like an undraped human figure (*tanquam veste detracta*). I am tempted to quote in this place the actual words employed by Peel about Cobden's eloquence : "It is the more to be admired because it is unaffected and unadorned."

must have been most exceptional. But he was wanting in quickness of perception. I remember his making a speech shortly before the Repeal of the Corn Laws; and on that occasion Peel, who seldom bestowed high praise, muttered, 'This is admirable.' But in this very speech Cobden went on to make use of a very unfortunate illustration : 'My honourable friend, the member for Rochdale, manufactures *long yarns* at a low price!'"

We talked about Bright; and I mentioned that I had heard his very fine speech at the dinner given to Mr. Garrison after the conclusion of the American Civil War. Mr. Gladstone rejoined that Bright approved of the American War, and seemingly of that war only. Bright had seen that, although the Northern States were not in the first instance consciously fighting against slavery, the practical result of the war would be to abolish slavery; and he had seen this when hardly anyone else did.

T.—"Do you suppose that the condition of the slaves was as bad as might be gathered from *Uncle Tom's Cabin* ?"

G.—"So far as physical suffering is concerned, I think the picture is too darkly coloured. Mrs. Beecher Stowe has combined all the worst details which were reported in various quarters. I will not say that she was morally to blame for this exaggeration; it was probably necessary for artistic effect. But I hold the great evil of slavery to have been, not physical suffering, but moral debasement. *It degrades God's human creatures below the human level.*" He also spoke of the bad effect on the masters, who were sinking lower and lower. I mentioned Chief Justice Shea, U.S.A., as having told me that the negroes are now becoming more and more helpless. Mr. Gladstone, after earnestly recapitulating the chief evils of slavery, such as the separation of families, etc., said that there was no doubt that it furnished some beautiful examples of faithful devotion. He confirmed the Chief Justice's opinion as to the present condition of the negroes, by the example of San Domingo, where they are reported (he believed on good authority) to be sinking into brutal idolatry, and even cannibalism. He said that evidence bearing in the same direction had been given him by a coloured President of the Liberian Republic. I reminded him that, twenty-eight years before, he had told me of some coloured man who had struck him, not merely by his intelligence, but also by his refined manners. He replied that this was probably the very man. He then suddenly looked startled, and exclaimed, " A formidable memory!" He went on to ask whether it was "a naturally strong memory which had been hardened and stimulated by practice." I compared it to a strong current which is made stronger by being forced to run in a narrow channel. My eyesight, I explained, limits the range of my reading, and cuts me off from the newspapers, and from many sources of observation. Thus my memory is concentrated upon a few subjects.

G.—" Archbishop Benson remarked to me in

conversation, that most men's memories are much impaired by the daily practice of reading the newspapers, and of skimming over a variety of unconnected subjects."

I asked him whether it was true that he ascribed his own good health to the practice of masticating his food twenty times. He said that, when his children were young, he told them that, when eating, they should think of four bars of common time written in quavers; by which, as he explained to my unmusical ear, he meant that they were to bite each mouthful thirty-two times; but he looked upon this as a counsel of perfection. He ate very slowly. I was surprised by this, as he talked so much. Montaigne, who never reached old age, had to increase mastication when he had passed middle life, and found it a bar to talking.

Mr. Gladstone added that he had other rules for the preservation of health. He felt the importance of Sunday rest. I asked, Did he get rest in listening to long sermons? He interrupted, "They are not often long now; but I do not like to hear more than one sermon which makes me think." He also found that a change of subjects was rest. He had acquired the power of keeping his mind off politics after he was in bed. When Bright was ill, he mentioned this to him. Bright rejoined, "This is just when I think of my speeches." He said that Bright's imprudence about health had been "abominable!" He thought that men of active minds and of a certain age would do well to consult some first-rate London doctor by way of taking preventive measures: "I do not say any doctor in particular; but let it be a first-rate one." I cross-questioned him further about Bright. He told me that Andrew Clark, when Bright went to consult him, asked, "To what do I owe the honour of seeing you?" Bright answered, "Mr. Gladstone made me come. He would give me no peace." After consulting Andrew Clark, he had no more of his nervous attacks. Mr. Gladstone added that he himself, under orders, had given up bitter beer, which he called a "divine drink" (θεῖον πότον).

I asked about Dizzy, and quoted this phrase, once used by him about the Liberal leaders when their Government had been beaten: "I see before me a range of extinct volcanoes."[1]

G.—"Dizzy did not show at his best during the last twenty years of his life. But he showed great ability when attacking Peel. Mind, I am not weighing his sayings in the moral scales; but they certainly showed great ability."

T.—"I understand that Sheil spoke of the falling

---

[1] I reported this incident to Mr. Gladstone as it had been told to me by a living statesman, who, I understood, had been present. Hayward gives a different account of it. He quotes the following extract from a speech delivered by Disraeli at Manchester: "As I sat opposite the Treasury bench, the Ministers reminded me of one of those marine landscapes not very unusual on the coasts of South America. You behold a range of exhausted volcanoes. Not a flame flickers on a single pallid crest. But the situation is still dangerous. There are occasional earthquakes, and ever and anon the dark rumbling of the sea." Can Dizzy have used this metaphor twice?

off of Disraeli's eloquence after Peel's death, and compared him to a dissecting surgeon without a corpse."

G.—"I will give one or two examples of his witty attacks on Peel. Speaking of the Maynooth Grant, he said of Peel: 'To what end is it that he thus convulses the country? That the Maynooth students may lie two in a bed instead of lying three in a bed.'[1] I will not deny that Maynooth was pauperised. But I will pass on to another example: Disraeli charged Peel with tracing the steam-engine back to the tea-kettle!"

I suppose that by this illustration Dizzy meant that Peel was too much in the habit of discussing political questions on first principles.

Mr. Gladstone went on to express surprise that the steam-engine was so long in being invented. I found that he did not know that there was a toy steam-engine in the Alexandrine Museum. He asked its date. I looked the question up, and afterwards informed him that Hero of Alexandria, in his *Pneumatica* (B.C. 130), says that he invented a steam apparatus for opening and shutting the great doors of a temple, and a toy globe which revolved by reaction from escaping steam.

He wanted to ask me about Butler, but remarked,

---

[1] Can Dizzy, when he used this metaphor, have been thinking of the son of the Vicar of Wakefield, who, being fain to embark on a tutorial career, was advertised of divers inconveniences of usherdom? "'Can you lie three in a bed?' 'No!' 'Then you won't do for a school.'"

with a smile, " I fear that the time is short, as the question comprises the whole of conduct. I don't wish to speak disrespectfully of a great critic; but, when Matthew Arnold speaks of conduct as comprising 75 per cent. of life, he seems to me to have spoken sheer nonsense."

T.—"Surely he did not intend it to be taken quite seriously."

G.—" Probably not; but, if he had not meant something, he would hardly have said it."

T.—" Do you mean that, in assigning three-quarters of life to conduct, he assigned too much or too little ? "

G.—" Too little. Conduct comprises the whole of life."

T.—" He divides the other quarter of life between Science and Art. Surely, therefore, when speaking of *conduct*, he uses the word in a technical sense as equivalent to *moral conduct*; he is referring to *le bien* as opposed to *le beau* and *le vrai.*"

Mr. Gladstone said that this was probably so; but he did not seem satisfied. He complained of my having spoken in *Stones of Stumbling* of Nature as being neither moral nor immoral, but " outside morality "; and asked how I applied this to the formation of good and bad habits. I said that the natural capacity of forming good habits, and the advantage resulting from their formation, may have been what Matthew Arnold had in view when he defined God as " the Eternal, not ourselves, that makes for righteousness." Mr. Gladstone seemed to dissent from that definition. Returning to the objection which he had made to my statement, that Nature is non-moral, I quoted Horace's well-known lines to the effect that piety grants no delay to wrinkles and old age. I insisted that, in regard to such visitations as earthquakes, and indeed to all agencies lying beyond human control, Nature is callously impartial in her treatment of good and bad men. The readers of the *Record* are, on an average, a more pious and praying class than the readers of the *Times*; and yet, after carefully studying the advertisements in these two journals, Mr. Francis Galton has discovered that the proportion of still births to ordinary births announced in the two journals is exactly the same; which is the more noteworthy as expectant mothers, in proportion as they are religious, are wont to be especially diligent in praying that their offspring may live. Mr. Gladstone's answer to me was on this wise: "Notwithstanding the apparently irregular distribution of temporal goods in this world, it is, I suppose, undeniable that godliness hath the promise of the life that now is, so far at least that good men, on the whole, have a happier lot than bad ones. If, in reply, we say that there are unexplained and grievous inequalities notwithstanding, may not the rejoinder be: (1) Philosophically, that it is unreasonable to suppose that the entire scheme of God's government would be within the comprehension of beings such as the

5

generality of men, or even of the most considerable;
(2) morally, in the words of Dante—

> ' Or tu chi sei, che vuoi sedere a scranna,
> Per giudicar da lungi mille miglia
> Con la veduta corta d'una spanna ? '

There is a very startling passage quoted by Southey
from John Wesley, in his *Life*, where Wesley
predicts that his followers, converted from vice
and ignorance to be sober and regular in life, will
infallibly become well-to-do, and will thereby fall
into a new set of dangers and temptations. Were
any man able humbly and intelligently to say that
he had been treated worse than he deserved, this
might be supposed to set up a case for him. But I
am not such a man, having been treated, not worse,
but far better; so that I cannot travel by his road,
even supposing it to be passable. The general
experience of mankind seems to offer a firmer basis
for indubitable argument than a comparison of the
advertisements in the *Record* or the *Times*. And, as
regards the *nec pietas moram*, surely it is undeniable
that what we call the virtuous man most commonly
lives longer than those of opposite character."

In this and other discussions with my revered
friend, I was naturally often the victim, not exactly
of an *argumentum ad verecundiam*, but of a *silentium ob verecundiam*. But naturally, also, my dim
religious awe of him has abated with time; and I
will therefore comment on one portion of what I
cannot but regard as his inconclusive reasoning. In
what sense can a man be treated by Providence

" worse " or " better " than he deserves ? The needs
of society compel us to annex suffering, not to all
sins, but to crimes, as a punishment, or rather as
a deterrent; but, apart from social needs, sin and
suffering are incommensurable quantities. Is it not,
therefore, as unmeaning to talk of an absolute relation between so much sin and so much suffering, or
between so much virtue and so much happiness, as
to talk of the distance between the 1st of January
and Westminster Bridge ?

Present politics, it will be seen, have been hitherto
barely touched upon. But, as Mr. Gladstone without
present politics seems like the play without the
part of Hamlet, I will here add that he afterwards
expressed his conviction to one of my guests that
at no distant time, not only will Home Rule in
Ireland have been carried, but people will have a
difficulty in understanding the state of mind which
postponed the carrying of it so long.

I asked Mr. Gladstone again about Marbot's
Memoirs; and we fell to talking of the first Napoleon,
for whom he entertained a quasi-admiration which
took me by surprise. An Epicurean God, if he had
deigned to bestow a thought on the inhabitants of
our planet, would doubtless have regarded Napoleon
as the Goliath of Lilliput, as the biggest ant in the
ant-hill, and, in a word, as somewhat less insignificant
and contemptible than his fellows. Such sages as
Bacon and Goethe would have shared this view to
the extent of thinking that, in our estimate of
human achievements generally, as in our estimate

of architecture, mere bulk must count for something. But a saint or a stern moralist would naturally have looked upon the great conqueror as a murderer on a huge scale, who ought to have been executed when convicted of his first crime. It was, therefore, very interesting to me to observe that Mr. Gladstone seemed to feel—what nearly all men of imagination sometimes feel—an odd sort of sympathy even with such greatness as Napoleon's: with greatness divorced from goodness, with force which not merely makes history exciting (*ut pueris placeas*) but also stirs up the stagnant pools of civilisation. I quoted to Mr. Gladstone the exclamation reported by Wellington as having been uttered by Talleyrand when someone, on hearing of Napoleon's death, called out, " Quel évènement ! " " Ce n'est plus un évènement," replied the master of epigram ; " Ce n'est qu'une nouvelle." Mr. Gladstone did not like this saying, which he criticised as follows :—" Your anecdote about Talleyrand is singularly illustrative of the man, and of the blinding power of a cynical habit of mind. See how this *nouvelle* struck Manzoni, who thus describes the blank left in the world by the departure of that Giant :—

> ' Ei fu ; Siccome immobile,
> Dato il mortal sospiro,
> Stette la spoglia immemore
> Orba di tanto spiro,
> Così *percossa, attonita,*
> *La terra* al nunzio sta ;
> Muta pensando all' ultima
> Ora dell' uom fatale,

> Nè sa quando una simile
> Orma di piè mortale
> La sua cruenta polvere
> A calpestar verrà.'

This is the noble beginning of Manzoni's noble ode called the *Cinque Maggio*."[1]

This ode of Manzoni on the death of Napoleon Mr. Gladstone pronounced to be the best thing that was written on the subject. He thought Byron's ode a failure; and, on my demurring, he said it was certainly not equal to Manzoni's. Goethe had paid Manzoni the compliment of translating the ode into German; but the translation was not equal to the original. At this point I cannot forbear asking: Was Talleyrand's exclamation really cynical? In saying that Napoleon's death, occurring when it did, was merely *une nouvelle*, he was speaking the exact truth. Was it ungenerous of him to give utterance to that truth? Or should we not rather say that he was pointing the finger, not at Napoleon in exile, but at the contrast between Napoleon in exile and Napoleon in power, and at the caprice of Fortune by which the bewildering change had been brought about? In fact, he was laying stress on the tragic pathos of the great Emperor's career, and indirectly at the fragility of human greatness (*Insignem attenuat Deus*). So that, when he thus contemplated

> "The Desolator desolate,
> The Victor overthrown"

---

[1] This ode was translated by Mr. Gladstone.

or, if you will, *Finem animæ quæ res humanas miscuit olim,* he was only expressing, in regard to Napoleon, the sentiment which Juvenal expressed about Hannibal, Johnson about Charles XII., and Scott about Richard I.—

> "He left a name at which the world grew pale,
>   To point a moral or adorn a tale."

January 2nd, 1893.—The Gladstones dined with us.

Mr. Gladstone never saw such a grand sea and such sheets of foam as on the shore of Biarritz; and he thought that, if Tennyson had seen it, he would have written about it.

He is of opinion that Professor Bryce, in his account of the social aspects of America, has not dwelt enough on the influence of wealth. He thinks that the "era of wealth," *i.e.* of colossal fortunes, is setting in; and he regrets it. He spoke of Mr. A—— as reported to have two and a half millions a year: "The Duke of Westminster is a pauper to him!" He expected that in a century's time the chief landed estates in England would still be intact. He spoke of one of his own farmers as beginning with a small farm and borrowing money to work it, and as now being able to pay his way. An Essex farmer had sent to Mr. Gladstone jars of jam in token of gratitude.

I spoke of genius as being often one-sided.

G.—"No.   Talent is; genius is not."

Seeing that I looked unconvinced, he asked me for an example of lopsided genius. I put the case of Milton.

G.—" Oh, he is an exception to all rules. He is an enigma—quite inexplicable."

He spoke in extremely strong terms against Milton's ideas of divorce which suited so ill with his Puritanism. He objected to the assertion in *Paradise Regained* that the Greeks had borrowed everything from the Jews. I remarked that even the greatest men are under the influence of the traditions of their time.

G.—" I cannot admit that about Milton. If he had consistently kept to those traditions, I would. But when he broke loose from them completely by writing as he did on divorce, he can no longer be excused on that ground."

I cited Shelley as a one-sided man of genius; but Mr. Gladstone declined to admit the validity of this instance, on the ground that Shelley, dying young, never quite " broke loose from the eggshell."

I was at the time preparing my article on " Sir Richard Owen and Old World Memories," which was afterwards published in the *National Review* (July 1893). Mr. Gladstone furnished me with a few reminiscences of Owen, which were inserted in the article by his kind permission. It is enough for my present purpose to mention that he said to me, in reference to Owen, that seldom, if ever, had any man of science left on his mind such an impression of genius—not talent merely, but genius. Darwin had struck him in the same sort of way; but Darwin he had only met once in society. And he went on to explain that on the comparative merits of the two men of science he offered no opinion; but that, so far as his personal observation was concerned, Owen was the one who seemed to him to bear the stamp of genius most unmistakably.

T.—"Would you not also say that Huxley is unmistakably a man of genius?"

G.—"Certainly not. Huxley has talent to any amount, but not genius. One of the younger men of science, Romanes, has struck me a good deal. I should say that *he* has genius."

With the greatest possible respect for Romanes, I was certainly startled at finding him (like the Prince Consort in the Albert Memorial) thus exalted over the heads of his fellows. The orthodox tendency of his later years may partly explain his being set above Huxley; but why did his distinguished critic prefer him even to those scientific men who were of the same way of thinking? May not this preference have been in some measure due to the fact that Mr. Gladstone regarded Romanes as, not merely a Christian, but as a proselyte, nay, as a re-converted pervert? In a word, is it not probable that there is joy among Anglicans over one heretic that recanteth more than over ninety and nine orthodox persons who need no recantation? Perhaps, after all, a recanting heretic is especially interesting because he is thought to be not quite safe,—to be, as it were, a brand *pluckable* from the burning.

It may be worth adding in this connexion that I

once heard Jowett express a doubt whether Mr. Gladstone himself could properly be called a man of genius. An orator of genius, he said, utters many words and phrases which linger in men's memory, and hardly any word or phrase so lingering has been uttered by Mr. Gladstone. Surely this is too narrow a test. The faculty of phrase-making is no more the touchstone of genius than is many-sidedness of mind in the signification which Mr. Gladstone would have attached to that term, a signification which somehow recalls the satirical saw, *Sapiunt, quia sentiunt mecum.*

But, after all, was not Jowett's criticism unjust to Mr. Gladstone in another way? Were all, or nearly all, the orator's characteristic sayings *writ in water*? Perhaps I am paradoxical; but I am inclined to think that the very popularity of some of his epigrammatic sallies may have lessened the permanent credit which he has obtained for them. It may be said of epigrams, as of marriageable daughters, that the cleverer and more pleasing they are, the sooner are they likely to be dissociated from the author of their being. At any rate, the most widely applicable and widely circulated epigrams of a talker or orator, as distinguished from those of a writer, are liable to be thus *de-personalised*. This may account for the fact that so many of Mr. Gladstone's phrases have, to employ the familiar hyperbole, become Iliads without a Homer. My meaning may be illustrated by his phrases, " the sorrowful evidence of indisputable fact," " prosperity advancing by leaps and bounds," and "turning out the Turks, bag and baggage"; by his (variously reported) assertion to the effect that Political Economy has now been relegated to the planet Saturn; and perhaps, too, by his allegation that a notorious event had brought a needful reform "within the range of practical politics." How many persons there are who, when they quote these and similar sayings of Mr. Gladstone, have no notion that it was he who uttered them! The division of the population into the "classes" and the "masses" is said to have been popularised, but not originated, by him. Its real author is apparently unknown. So that here we have a wholly de-personalised epigram; it has paid for its popularity by anonymity. Let me add that Mr. Gladstone's own expression that England is guarded by a "streak of silver sea" is often fathered on the Shakespearean John of Gaunt. This patriotic exclamation, or, as St. Paul would have said, this "confident boasting" of his, may suggest another reflection. It is obvious to remark that the watery bulwark which he so highly valued would be, metaphorically as well as literally, under-mined by the Channel Tunnel for which, as we shall see presently, he was so eager. Indeed, it must be understood, once for all, that I am not raising the question whether the Gladstonian apothegms to which I have referred were wisely and seasonably uttered. All I insist on is that they are "such stuff" as proverbs are made of; in other words, they have something about them which has brought them into social currency; and they have continued in circulation, not because of the famous image and superscription which they originally bore, but even after that image and superscription had been gradually effaced.[1]

Mr. Gladstone said that the Church of England took its form from Henry VIII., Elizabeth, and Laud. He thought little of Cranmer on account of his moral weakness; and not much of Latimer. He said that Latimer, when a Catholic, preached a sermon while a man was being roasted on a slow fire.

G.—"I have a weakness for Latimer, all the same."

Thinking this too little praise for Latimer, I gave him (as the phrase goes) "a strange bed-fellow," by saying that I had a weakness for Charles I.

G.—"So have I, although he was unfortunately such a liar!"

I remarked that Shakespeare, if it had been his supreme misfortune to be one of the Stuart kings, might have found no opening for his dramatic genius, and might now be remembered only as uniting the faults of Charles I. and Charles II. The indifference with which he refers to Prince John's treatment of the rebels in *Henry IV*. Part II. shows that he had some sympathy with the view that no

---

[1] I have lately come across a remarkable passage which gives independent, if somewhat indirect, support to the general view set forth in this paragraph. "A writer," says Johnson, "who obtains his full purpose loses himself in his own lustre. . . . Of an art universally practised, the first teacher is forgotten."

engagement was binding between a king and rebel subjects.

G.—"I quite agree with you; indeed, I will go further. Shakespeare seems to me to have been a worshipper of the Tudor despotism. I say this with deep regret. The three great poets of the world would, I think, generally be admitted to be Homer, Dante and Shakespeare; the Germans would add Goethe. The morality of Dante is always pure and good. Homer, too, seems always to throw our sympathies on the right side."

I demurred, and mentioned the case of Dolon.

G.—"That was a night march, and it was necessary to meet stratagem by stratagem."

T.—"Diomed and Ulysses virtually promised Dolon his life, and should have spared him."

G.—"We must make allowance for the morality of Homer's day, and the little value that was then set on human life."

To me it seems that the principle that he thus called to his aid is of such wide application that, if it proves anything, it proves more than he intended. Either men of genius are bound to rise above the moral standard of their age, or they are not. If they are, why excuse Homer? If they are not, why condemn Shakespeare?

Mr. Gladstone said that Sir Henry Taylor, in his *Correspondence*, spoke of Walter Scott's moral judgments as being sound, but feeble. In explanation of this, Mr. Gladstone added that, while setting the power of delineating character above any other, he himself thought that it tended to give such "objectivity" to the view of moral and immoral conduct as to weaken the sense of sin. He promised to send me the reference to the passage in Taylor's *Correspondence*; and, as will be seen further on, he kept his word.

In return, I drew his attention to the following observations of Ruskin :—

"It was necessary he [Shakespeare] should lean *no* way ; that he should contemplate with absolute equality of judgment the life of the court, cloister, and tavern, and be able to sympathise so completely with all creatures as to deprive himself, together with his personal identity, even of his conscience, as he casts himself into their hearts. He must be able to enter into the soul of Falstaff or Shylock with no more sense of contempt or horror than Falstaff or Shylock themselves feel for or in themselves. He must be utterly without anger, utterly without purpose ; for if a man has any serious purpose in life, that which runs counter to it, or is foreign to it, will be looked at frowningly or carelessly by him."

T.—"Do you not call this passage interesting ?"

G.—"I call it, not interesting merely, but wonderful."

I spoke of Tennyson's admiration for the passage in *Paradise Lost* about "Tammuz," and for the line—

"Of Abana and Pharphar, lucid streams."

In regard to this line, Mr. Gladstone agreed with Tennyson, and he went on to quote with sonorous enthusiasm his favourite line in the Odyssey—

"μηδέ τι χείρονος ἀνδρὸς ἐϋφραίνοιμι νόημα,"

and spoke of this as specially fine, because the sentiment is expressed by a woman. Clearly, however, the sentiment is not Penelope's, but Homer's. Would there not have been more point in Mr. Gladstone's remark if he had agreed with Mr. Samuel Butler in thinking that the *Odyssey* was written by a woman?

He never quite forgave Walter Scott for the part he took about Queen Caroline's trial, or for his somewhat servile loyalty to "that creature George IV." Also he regarded Scott's Toryism as "silly." I asked whether such Toryism was not inevitable in such an admirer of antiquity. In reply, he expressed a wish that modern Conservatives had a greater love of antiquity. Lord Salisbury had broken too much from old traditions in being at once Prime Minister and Foreign Secretary, and also in making Huxley a Privy Councillor. Mr. Gladstone would have preferred some other form of distinction for the great biologist. He was angry with the Conservatives for distributing G.C.B.'s broadcast before leaving office, among men who had no claim to them, and did not expect them. He said that the Liberals were equally wanting in respect for antiquity; but this was excusable in them—such a defect was their besetting sin.

I dined with Mr. and Mrs. Gladstone.

I quoted the Basque proverb, that "the needle, which clothes others, remains naked itself"; and applied it to France, which, while herself subject to Louis Napoleon, gave free institutions to Italy. He approved of the comparison, and went on to speak of the dangers of the Republic. But he remarked that each form of government since the Revolution had lasted longer than the one before. (He cannot have counted the Republic of 1848.) I said that Charles Austin used to maintain that France had lost her best chance of good government when she got rid of Louis Philippe. Mr. Gladstone said that he was inclined to judge Louis Philippe severely, as having been narrow-minded. I spoke of his Ministers, and asked whether they were not responsible for the faults of his reign. Mr. Gladstone thought that they had acted under royal pressure, and that if Leopold had been their king the course of French history might have been different.

I asked him what value he attached to the study and composition of Latin and Greek verses. I told him that Goethe advised everyone to repeat a few stanzas of good poetry daily, and added that I myself repeated one of Horace's Odes daily. He advised me to set about translating them into English verse. He had done so quite recently.

A friend of Bagehot's once said of Mr. Gladstone, " He may be a good Christian, but he is an atrocious pagan." The word " pagan " is here used in a good sense. And, when it was denied that Mr. Gladstone was a good pagan, it was meant that he was not marked, as most Englishmen and philosophers of all countries are marked, by that dislike of extremes, and by those self-sufficing and self-restraining qualities which go to make up the " magnanimous man" portrayed by Aristotle. He was no doubt open to this charge; yet even in him the wholesome pagan ingredient was not quite wanting. His continued study of Horace proves this. To study Horace is to learn *nil admirari*; and the prolonged effort of translating him must serve to dilute Christian with pagan modes of feeling.

Mr. Gladstone found that he could write Latin verses at least as well at sixty as when he was a young man. But he had since given it up. He was in favour of keeping up Latin verses, but was not eager for compulsory English verses. He spoke of Charles Wesley as having written 120,000 lines of English verse—more than all the great epic poems of the world put together. He said there was a difference of opinion about how much Wesley had written; but he thought that 4000 hymns was a low estimate, and each of them he computed at thirty lines on an average. He thought him a much over-rated writer, "Wrestling Jacob" being the only one he cared for.

Does "Wrestling Jacob," I would ask, deserve the praise it so often receives? Does not this versified allegory, even more than the doxology after the Psalms, impress one as a sort of Vandalism, or, at least, as a jarring anachronism, by engrafting the highly-developed Catholic theology on one of the very oldest and rudest of Israelitish stocks?

I mentioned that it was my habit to repeat Tennyson's "St. Agnes' Eve," and the canto of "In Memoriam" beginning "O yet we trust," on Sundays. This canto expresses my religious aspirations better than anything else. He asked me, evidently with an implied negative (equivalent to the Latin *Num*) discernible in his voice, whether I thought Tennyson a philosopher. I replied that our aspirations point to the conclusion that all evil may be educative. He hinted at the difficulty involved in the pain suffered by the lower animals, and said that he considered " the existence of evil inexplicable."

I could not help calling to mind the considerations commonly adduced to prove the indispensability of evil—considerations to the effect that "the rays of happiness, like those of light, are colourless when unbroken," and that even the horticulture of Eden would have grown wearisome without the snake. Or perhaps it would be a juster as well as a more pleasing metaphor to say that the world, like the water of Bethesda, has to be troubled in order that its latent virtue may be drawn out. But I felt that every such supposition must, at bottom, rest on the assumption that the Deity is limited in power, and that to Mr. Gladstone's mind the notion of such Divine limitation would be abhorrent.

I asked him what he thought of Professor Mivart's article in the *Nineteenth Century*, called " The Happiness in Hell."

G.—"If a man begins by being tipsy sometimes, and ends by being dead drunk daily,—if he begins by beating his wife, and ends by killing her, I see no reason to think he will begin to improve as soon as he dies."

I remarked that Dives is represented as testifying
6

when in " torments," a sympathy with his surviving kinsfolk ; but I added that I did not pretend to draw from this expression of sympathy the hopeful conclusion that many Broad Churchmen draw, namely, that he was not in Hell, but in Purgatory.

G.—" I look upon Dives as a very mild instance. As landlords go, he was above the average ; he *did* let Lazarus have of his superfluities."

Mr. Gladstone went on to hint that his case was not represented as beyond hope. I said that surely the text about the impassable gulf suggested the idea that Dives' doom was final ; but Mr. Gladstone was not convinced. His last words about it were, " I will give you something to think over—*Have time and space any existence outside the human intelligence?*" "Unquestionably," I replied, "they exist for the animal intelligence." He said that he regarded that as the same thing on a small scale. And then came the final " God bless you."

I had a talk with Mr. Gladstone in which he told me that he wished above all things to keep up righteous indignation. I replied that anyone who studied heredity, and felt how much some people are handicapped in the moral race, can hardly keep up an acute sense of sin ; and on that account I excused the deficiency of that sense in Shakespeare and Scott. He said that he did not see that Shakespeare and Scott were students of heredity, or that Shakespeare, at any rate, seemed at all conscious of the moral difficulties connected with it. I could not help

thinking that, in speaking thus, he went too far.
In *Antony and Cleopatra*, Lepidus says of Antony's
faults that they are "hereditary rather than purchased; what he cannot change, than what he chooses."
So, too, Hamlet cites the case of certain men having

> "Some vicious mole of nature in them,
> As in their birth (wherein they are not guilty,
> Since nature cannot choose his origin)."

But it should be observed that, in these passages,
Shakespeare seems to limit the plea of heredity to
the case of venial faults, and that he fails to realise
the full force of the difficulty. On the other hand,
Tennyson felt the difficulty in its widest scope, as is
shown in the following passage, which he puts into
the mouth of the cultivated villain in "The Promise
of May":—

> "He was only
> A poor philosopher who called the mind
> Of children a blank page, a *tabula rasa.*
> There, there, is written in invisible ink
> Lust, Prodigality, Covetousness, Craft,
> Cowardice, Murder—and the heat and fire
> Of life will bring them out, and black enough,
> So the child grow to manhood."

I reminded Mr. Gladstone of the story that
Baxter, seeing a criminal on his way to execution,
exclaimed, "There, but for the grace of God, goes
Richard Baxter!" I remarked that I had heard
a like saying ascribed to Sir Matthew Hale.

Mr. Gladstone believed that its date was farther
back, and that its author was Bradford, the martyr
under Queen Mary. The saying points to the con-

clusion that men are to a great extent the creatures of circumstance. Our conversation was thus brought back to the perennial suit in the Court of Morality, which may be designated as the case of Necessity *versus* Responsibility. Mr. Gladstone had once significantly exhorted me to be careful not to blunt my sense of sin; and I thought that he scarcely understood the process by which the "smiling toleration" commended by Goethe forces itself upon some naturally rigid moralists in their own despite. I was anxious to illustrate clearly my point of view; and I therefore (in biblical phrase) "took up my parable" as follows: Let us start with the supposition—no matter how extravagant—that a band of Anarchists, incensed against their leading countrymen, revenge themselves by kidnapping many infant sons of bishops, statesmen, and even princes; that the poor children, captured too young to retain any recollection of their home and parentage, are brought up to prefer evil to good; and that their corruptors, by dexterous lying, inoculate them with a rancorous hatred against peaceful, and especially against rich citizens. Let it be also assumed that the bereaved parents suppose that their lost ones have been accidentally killed in some manner (as by drowning in the sea), which would account for the disappearance of their bodies, and that they are gradually consoled by reflecting that some at least of their other sons bid fair to earn credit and distinction. Let us now skip twenty or thirty years, and imagine that, just when those early promises of credit and distinction are beginning to be realised, some atrocious murders are brought home to youths who look as if Nature had designed them for better things; and that, as soon as sentence of death has been . passed on the offenders, the original kidnappers, from some safe hiding-place, let it be known that those felons of aristocratic mien are the sons of distinguished parents, and are kinsmen—in a few instances, perhaps, twin-brothers —of some of the most rising men in the country. The law would presumably be left to take its course; but the irresponsible murderers (so to call them) would excite compassion rather than indignation. They would be thought to have sinned, and to be about to suffer, as it were by accident. Nor would compassion be limited to these particular offenders. Presently, what may be called the intellectualising but demoralising question would begin to be asked: May not many of our worst criminals be men who, but for a caprice of fortune, would have given proof of possessing true hearts and " hands that the rod of empire might have swayed "? And thus life would come to be regarded as a cruel farce, in which the players act by compulsion, and every player who has to act a villain's part is punished for the villain's crimes. Thus, we seem to be in a vicious circle from which there is no escape. If we acknowledge with Madame de Staël that " Tout comprendre, c'est tout pardonner," we are bound to add "Tout pardonner, c'est éteindre la morale."

After first listening with exemplary patience to

what may be termed these parabolic reflections, and then expressing a doubt whether Madame de Staël meant her *mot* to be taken quite literally, Mr. Gladstone went on to say: "I will go the length of admitting that, even in the extreme case of pronouncing the sentence of death, a judge, if he is really a Christian man, will be liable to say to himself, 'God knows how much that man has been tempted, and though for the sake of society I am bound to punish him, he may on the Judgment Day be preferred before me.'"

I rejoined that many modern thinkers would hold that, if full allowance were made for heredity, education and temptation, then judge, criminal, and everyone else would stand exactly on a level. When a man has been thoroughly worsted by another in the moral race, may we not assume that he has laboured under a corresponding disadvantage? nay, that the extent of the defeat is exactly measured by the amount of the handicap?

G.—"No; I cannot admit that."

In illustration of the view to which he was opposed, I am tempted to mention that, in one of the most "modern" of Lucian's Dialogues, the ghost of an outrageous criminal, after being condemned to the most varied and unremitting tortures that the nether regions can provide, sets up the plea that he was throughout the victim of Destiny; and Minos is at his wits' end to know how to deal with him.

Reverting to a topic referred to in a former conversation, I spoke about the immense popularity which was at the time achieved by Sheridan's Begum Speech, and which modern readers find it hard to understand. Can that speech have been well reported?

G.—"Has any speech of that time, any speech (for example) of either of the Pitts, been well reported? The younger Pitt is chiefly known, as an orator, for his happy quotations. When contemplating retirement from office, he applied to himself Horace's

> " probamque
> Pauperiem sine dote quaero "—

the preceding clause, " mea Virtute me involvo," being conspicuous by its omission.

He applied most unjustly to Ireland and England the lines about being under equal laws; and there was also the quotation from Virgil which he introduced into his speech against the slave trade." [1]

I reminded him that Pitt quoted the stanza, beginning *Duris ut ilex,* in reference to the attempts made by Napoleon to weaken Great Britain by injuring

---

[1] " He [Pitt] burst as it were into a prophetic vision of the civilisation that shall dawn upon Africa, and recalled the not less than African barbarism of heathen Britain ; exclaiming, as the first beams of the morning sun pierced the windows of Parliament, and appeared to suggest the quotation :—

> 'Nos . . . primus equis Oriens afflavit anhelis,
> Illic sera rubens accendit lumina Vesper.' "
>
> LORD ROSEBERY'S *Pitt.*

The point of comparison seems to have been that the blessing of freedom was granted to the English at the dawn of their history, but that it was being vouchsafed to the negroes only at the eleventh hour

her colonies and her trade. He regretted that no such quotations are given or would be understood now.

He said that he was "suffused with shame" about the conduct of the English in regard to the Channel Tunnel. It used to be said that the opposition to it came from one man, namely, Lord Palmerston. But then the panic arose. At the request of the English Government, the French took great trouble to make inquiries as to the practicability of the scheme.

G.—"We English plume ourselves on our common sense, and are never tired of laughing at the frivolity and vacillation of the French. But, since the Norman Conquest, the English have invaded France at least ten times as often as the French have invaded England. And yet the English now raise this outcry about the risk of a French invasion."

I put in a word about the French conscription, and about their army being now much stronger than ours.

"From your speaking in that way," he said, with a smile, "I see what line you are disposed to take about the tunnel."

The orator in him came out when he made the somewhat extravagant statement, that Pius IX. was more ignorant than he thought any educated man could be; for his Holiness had said that there were half a million of Catholics in Glasgow. I imagine that his Holiness, if Mr. Gladstone rightly understood him, must have confounded the number of Catholics in Glasgow with that of the entire population. Mr. Gladstone surprised me by knowing accurately the population of Liverpool, and the number of Catholics there. He appeared to think that, if the Scotch Kirk were disestablished, the result might be a fusion of the three Presbyterian bodies.

He seemed irritated with the German writers, who taught that the Iliad and the Odyssey were made up, as he said, "of a fortuitous concourse of atoms." Goethe never favoured this view. Mr. Gladstone went on to advert to the extreme clumsiness of German prose, always excepting that of a few great writers. He spoke of German prose as being "worthy of African savages." Being asked how he explained this, he compared the German prose of the present day to the English prose of two or three centuries ago. I said that Matthew Arnold spoke of the function of the eighteenth century in England as being to create a prose literature. He replied that he did not know that Matthew Arnold had said this; but that he quite agreed.

A propos of modern views on eternal punishment, he pronounced the besetting sins of rationalistic writers to be "negation and timidity." I objected that in Mr. John Morley and others we find negation, but certainly not timidity. He said that he was not speaking of such men, and did not use the word "negation" in that sense. He seemed to use the word as equivalent to a conscious or unconscious moral scepticism.

He again gave utterance to the opinion expressed by him in a former conversation, that Matthew Arnold ought to have represented conduct as comprising, not only three-quarters of life, but the whole of it. In vindication of the great critic, I reminded Mr. Gladstone that he himself in his Romanes Lecture had ranked Bacon among those of whom Cambridge ought to be proud. Now, if conduct comprises the whole of life, every man ought to be judged by an exclusively moral standard; and, if Bacon were so judged, Cambridge would have no cause to be proud of him. His title to admiration is based on that portion—Matthew Arnold would say that fourth part—of life which lies outside the domain of morality. This "wisest, brightest, meanest of mankind" is more praised for his wisdom and brightness than he is condemned for his meanness. As a schoolboy might say, he obtained more marks for his Philosophical papers and his Essays, than his virtuous contemporaries obtained for their good conduct.

Mr. Gladstone replied that he had only been assigning to Bacon his rank in respect of ability. But I could not see that this met the difficulty. Cambridge would not have cause to be proud of having produced a very able conspirator or traitor.

Mr. Gladstone went on to say that, when he gave the Romanes Lecture, he thought that before this century Cambridge had had the distinct advantage in regard to poets; but Mr. Arthur Galton had given instances of Cambridge poets who took a dislike to Cambridge, and in some cases preferred Oxford. He said that Dryden spoke, in this relation, of going from Thebes to Athens; and he wondered, if, in thus giving the palm to Oxford, Dryden was a liar, or, as he expressed it, "a rogue." He expressed great admiration for Dryden's power of arguing in verse, as shown in "The Hind and Panther." He spoke of Thomas Cromwell as a wonderful man, though "something of a rogue." He had never heard the famous answer in an examination to the question, "What do you know of Oliver Cromwell?" "He cut off his king's head, and usurped the kingdom. Afterwards he was filled with remorse, and exclaimed, when dying, 'Would that I had served my God as I have served my king!'"

The conversation passed on to the subject of Malapropisms, which seemed to amuse Mr. Gladstone. Someone mentioned that a lady friend, observing that one of her horses was in much better condition than his mate, was told by the groom, "This one *domesticates* his food better than the other." This was capped by the true story of the lady, who, having complained to her butcher that the meat he had sent her was high, was met with the surprised and surprising rejoinder, "You *putrefy* me with amazement!"

I called Mr. Gladstone's attention to a line in Milton's translation of the Ode *Quis multa gracilis*—

> "Who, always vacant, always amiable,
>   Hopes thee"

and I expressed an opinion that an inverted sentence of this kind is less plain in English than in Latin. This led on to Mr. Gladstone's saying that he was in favour of original classical compositions; but he owned to having some misgivings.

He regarded with "mingled jealousy and admiration" the purity of Bright's English, but said that Bright had once fallen into one of the "worst of vulgarisms"; Bright used the verb "to transpire" in the sense of "to occur." Mr. Gladstone remarked that "transpire" properly meant "to ooze out." I reminded him that "to perspire" in French was "transpirer," and was surprised to find that this was news to him.

He was struck by the way in which some eminent scholars who were also masters of English, such as Roundell Palmer, showed no classical flavour in their English compositions. Lowe was a great exception to this.

G.—"If people went into an extreme about Classics, the last half of the nineteenth century has gone into just as great an extreme about modern languages. I believe that science will be the great instrument of education in the future. You may find something to suit all intellectual needs in the various sciences from Astronomy to—what shall I say?"

T.—"To Gastronomy?"

G. (*smiling*)—"No—to Embryology."

He said that he had called Mill the "Saint of Rationalism," and gave as an example of his saintliness that, when a rather bitter attack had been made

on him by Lowe in a debate on reform, he attempted
no retort, but merely confined himself to the point
at issue. I referred to the lady who, after talking
to Littré, said, "Je viens de parler à un saint qui ne
croit pas en Dieu." Mr. Gladstone laughed and said,
"Yes; but I have the advantage of priority. This is
not a case of *Pereant qui nostra ante nos dixerint.*
How trying that sort of thing is!"

T.—"*Pereant qui nostra* post *nos dixerint.* This
seems to me to represent a state of things more
trying still;—when one has originated an idea, and
some more conspicuous person cribs it, and gets the
credit for it."

December 30th, 1893.—It may be convenient here
to insert some notes of a conversation with Mr.
Gladstone with which a learned divine, who lives
near Biarritz, has kindly furnished me:—

"Mr. Gladstone talked a little on the general
principles of Political Economy. On the actual
distribution of wealth he felt uneasy, and he thought
that the irresponsibility in the condition of holding
wealth nowadays, especially in the United States,
and the difficulty or impossibility of bringing home
to men the responsibility of riches held under their
present conditions, was the black spot in the
future.

"The history of Ireland, he said, was unlike that
of any other nation. The oppression of it by England had not been the oppression of a race who had
once been conquerors or dangerous; like that of the

Poles by Russians, or of the Moors by Spaniards. The Irish had done nothing to warrant the oppression: they were only reclaiming that of which they had been gratuitously deprived, and we owe them restoration of the theft.

"He told me about the difficulty which he felt in making his ecclesiastical appointments; he had always endeavoured in parishes to find the best man to carry on the work on the general lines of his predecessor. He was anxious not to appoint a High Churchman to a Low Church parish, nor *vice versâ*. But it was very difficult to tell how a man would be received, or how he might turn out. He instanced his appointment of Dr. L—— to the parish of ——. He thought that he had got the very man to follow a good evangelical, with hearty services. To his surprise he received a deputation, with the late incumbent at the head, and a petition with 2000 signatures, protesting against the appointment. He appealed privately to Dr. L—— to resign, promising some compensatory post, and offering pecuniary indemnity for his expenses. But Dr. L—— said that he had gone too far to retire with honour, and that his friends in the neighbourhood assured him that the opposition was factitious, and that the majority of the parish was not averse to him. So Mr. Gladstone yielded. A year afterwards he found the Doctor most popular, with a crowded church, hearty services, and not above twenty malcontents in the parish.

"He spoke much of the superficiality of popular

writing on Theology, and of the ordinary sermons, especially those of the Low Church school. The teaching was so loose and vague; it gave nothing to do, no rule of conduct. 'Only believe all is right with you, and all will somehow come right at the last.' Many High Churchmen preached more really evangelical sermons than the Low Churchmen did. The popular teaching on Eschatology was most superficial. He praised Mr. Oxenham's book on the subject much, and called it logical and convincing. Universalism really implied dualism; and it was no vindication to say that in the final casting up of accounts the balance would be found on the side of good. Annihilation could not be the end. The real problem was that of the origin and existence of evil, not its extinction; and this problem was wholly insoluble by man. The unfallen angels and spirits showed that evil was not a necessity, or a necessary condition of created existence.

"He agreed that all human knowledge was relative; religious knowledge being no more absolute than any other. Newman was not great as a philosopher; but in spiritual matters, and in the knowledge of and the power of probing the human heart. He spoke indignantly of the prosecutions of Ritualists by the Church Association. They were a failure always, whether won or lost. They provoked reaction, and produced what they were intended to stop. He hoped that there would be no more of them, and that the bishops would stop them by their veto. In answer to a suggestion that there should be Standing Committees of Convocation something like the Congregations and the Holy Office at Rome, not to judge individuals, but to decide on the questions and abstract cases submitted to them, he said that the difficulty would be to find a body of theologians in the English Church whose decisions or opinions would inspire sufficient respect.

" He was asked if he had observed the singular absence of the sense of sin in the works of American divines of all schools. 'Ah,' said he slowly, 'the sense of sin—that is the great want in modern life; it is wanting in our sermons, wanting everywhere!' This was said slowly and reflectively, almost like a monologue.

" Then he talked of Driver's criticism of the 51st Psalm to the effect that it could not be by David because of the verse, 'Against Thee, Thee only have I sinned.' He had injured Uriah and Bathsheba.

" *G.*—' Where sin against God is really felt, *that* absorbs the other. Any sin against man is light in comparison of the sin against God.'

" He agreed that *Against Thee, etc.,* is the correlative of *Who can forgive sins but God only ?* [1]

" Mr. Gladstone's attention was next called to D. G. Azcarates' *Discurso* in Spanish at the *Ateneo* of Madrid. The writer speaks of Mr. Gladstone as crowning his unparalleled career by bringing home the responsibilities of wealth to Londoners. Mr. Glad-

---

[1] Is not more conclusive evidence of the post-Davidic, or rather post-Exilian, date of the Psalm furnished by the phrase, "Build Thou the walls of Jerusalem"? (L.A.T.)

stone said that this is not so much needed in London as in the United States: in London they are becoming aware of the responsibility attaching to riches."

The friend who has supplied me with the foregoing materials concludes with this comment :—

" My impressions of last year as to Mr. Gladstone's earnest piety, immense range of thought and learning, and wonderful physical power, and of the persuasive management of his voice, were but heightened this year. He would have been a great theologian if he had not been so great a statesman."

January 24*th*, 1894.—Mr. and Mrs. Gladstone dined with us.

I said that I supposed that there were more means for the endowment of research in Germany than in England. Mr. Gladstone rejoined that he thought that the collective sum from which such men as Wordsworth and Tennyson received pensions was £30,000 a year. I called attention to the increased endowment of research at Oxford. He spoke of it as strange that in no other country were there such large sums for the endowment of education, and yet there is no country where education is so expensive. He believed that Eton was more expensive now than in his younger days, and that Harrow was more expensive still. In the case of Eton, the *modus operandi* of the change was through the masters more and more encroaching on the dames. Being asked whether he did not think that the reason was

7

that it was wished to make public schools the especial resort of gentlemen's sons, he said, " No, no ; it is very disgraceful, but not quite so bad as that."   I quoted Renan's saying to the effect that there is no second-rate University in Germany, with its " Professeurs hâves et faméliques," which has not done more for intellectual progress than the great aristocratic University of Oxford, " avec ses revenues immenses, ses collèges splendides, ses *Fellows* paresseux."   He did not agree.   " I don't believe a word of it," he said.   In confirmation, however, of Renan's opinion, which was also Mark Pattison's, I will quote a passage from Bagehot, who considered the *Saturday Review*, whose contributors in his time were mainly University men, to be a sort of thermometer indicating the moral temperature of our English Universities.   He says of that Journal :—

" We may search and search in vain through this repository of the results of ' University teaching ' for a single truth which it has established, for a single high cause which it has advanced, for a single deep thought which is to sink into the mind of its readers. We have, indeed, a nearly perfect embodiment of the corrective scepticism of a sleepy intellect."

Mr. Gladstone quoted a saying of Napoleon from Taine's posthumous volume : " Je ne crois pas aux religions ; mais qui a fait tout ceci ? . . . les prêtres valent mieux que les Cagliostro, les Kant, et tous les rêveurs d'Allemagne."   He chuckled over the reference to Kant.   He said : " When next I see Lord Acton, I mean to quote this to him.   He is a great admirer of Kant's writings, and it will be good for him to be told what Napoleon thought of them! Generally, when I try to surprise him by a quotation, he tells me exactly where it comes from."

He repeated a passage from another French writer in reference to Napoleon : " Nous avons assez entendu parler du Fils de l'Homme ; mais Napoléon était l'Homme lui-même."

G.—" He put him far above our Saviour."

The book increased Mr. Gladstone's sense of Napoleon's supreme greatness, but did not raise his view of the Emperor's moral character.

He spoke of Pearson's *National Life and Character.* He seemed especially interested in the author's statement that the crowding of men in big towns may force on State Socialism ; but he agreed with me that Pearson's own sympathies were in favour of Individualism, State Socialism being at best a necessary evil. I objected to Pearson's notion that Western Europe would ever allow itself to be encroached upon and practically overwhelmed by immigrants from the yellow races. Would not our descendants defend themselves by arms? They might vindicate such a summary proceeding by saying (in dog Latin) *salus civilizationis, suprema lex.* Mr. Gladstone, however, laughed at the idea of our descendants taking refuge in strong measures: " If the cultivated races cannot defend themselves without appealing to brute force, God help them !"

I said that I used to write in preference-books, that I wished that my lot could have been thrown in the distant future, but that now I am satisfied with the nineteenth century.

G.—" I should have chosen the time of Homer."

We spoke of the conservative tendency of such pessimistic views as Pearson's; and Mr. Gladstone went on to say that he thought he remembered the account that I had given of my own views in my article on my father a year or two earlier,[1] but he was afraid of misquoting me. I replied that I thought that he was paying me the greatest possible compliment in remembering anything about it. He seemed not to approve of my Whiggism. I explained that by education, tradition and temperament I am strongly Conservative; but that I call myself Con-servative," not *a* Conservative. He admitted that he also was Conservative in a certain sense. I spoke of the Conservative influence of ladies' society. He demurred to the implied statement that women are more Conservative than men. He should rather describe them as "more emotional." He, however, agreed that they are more under the influence of the clergy. I spoke of women's influence at municipal elections and at elections for the school board. He doubted whether their influence is Conservative in either of these cases. But he said that the women chosen are scarcely typical women. I quite agreed; but I explained that I was referring to the influence of the many women who vote at these elections, and not of the few who are elected.

[1] "Lord Tollemache and His Anecdotes," *Fortnightly Review*, July 1892.

From clever women in general, the conversation passed on to George Eliot. Mr. Gladstone considered her rather a man than a woman. *Silas Marner* is the work of hers that he most admired. But he complained that her novels " were out of tune." I remarked that at the end of the seventh of the eight parts in which *Middlemarch* first appeared, one hoped that Dorothea would marry Lydgate. Mr. Gladstone intimated his assent.

He told me that his great admiration for Scott was tempered by regret that he was weighed down by so much inferior work. A similar criticism he applied to Shakespeare, though in a less degree. I spoke of Lord Lytton's portraiture (in *The Last of the Barons*) of Gloucester (Richard III.), and especially of Warwick, as more lifelike than Shakespeare's. To my surprise Mr. Gladstone seemed not to know who the last of the Barons was. He pleaded that it was doubtful whether the latter part of Henry VI. was by Shakespeare, but admitted that there is something very arbitrary in the way in which critics decide by internal evidence what is Shakespeare's and what is not.

He said that his favourites among Scott's novels were *Kenilworth* and the *Bride of Lammermoor*. I asked whether he did not find the bad endings of these two novels depressing.

G.—" I don't mind that in such works of art as these."

I told him that the *Bride of Lammermoor* was also Jowett's favourite.

G.—" I am very glad to hear it; and I will quote the statement on your authority." He went on to say that the three novels of Scott which are generally the most popular are *Ivanhoe, Old Mortality* and *Waverley*. He ranked those next to the two others. Returning to George Eliot, he surprised me by saying that he had never read *Daniel Deronda*. Something was said about George Eliot's enthusiasm for the Jews, which at last became almost as vehement as Disraeli's. Both those writers sometimes leave the impression of looking forward to the restoration of the old Hebrew Monarchy. Might they not (adapting Virgil) have taken for their motto : *Jam redit et David, redeunt Solomonia regna* ?

Hence we drifted into the Germans' hatred of the Jews.

G.—" I used to think the Irish the most oppressed people on earth; but now I think that the Jews have been even more oppressed. I believe that Döllinger wrote in favour of the Jews; and I thought it very creditable of him to do so. I understand that the kings in the Middle Ages, including even King John, often took the part of the Jews against the nobles. Was it because they wished to save the Jews from oppression ? Nothing of the sort. But they considered that the right to torture a Jew and to extort money from him ought to be a monopoly of their own." He did not deny that the Jews had their faults. After praising Finlay's *History* in high terms, he said that he

had there learnt that towards the end of the Middle
Ages the Greek Christians had a bad time of it ; for,
while the Mahometans hated them as infidels, and the
Catholics hated them as heretics, the Jews took advantage of their weakness to settle old scores with them.

G.—" Lord Acton is writing a history of Liberty,
and I shall be anxious to see how he will treat the
question of the Jews."

T.—" In writing such a work, is he not likely to
get into trouble with the Roman authorities ? "

G.—" His work may be put on the *Index* ; but
that is all. They will never excommunicate an
English Peer. I always say that, if Lord Acton had
written what Döllinger has written, and *vice versâ*,
it would still have been the Professor who would
have got into trouble, while the Peer would have
escaped scot free."

We talked about the old Greeks.

G.—" I am a great admirer of the old Olympian
religion, as it was set forth by the supreme genius
of Homer. It was quite different in the hands of
the later Greeks; and the mythology of the Roman
poets serves as an opaque curtain which hides it
from us. Do the Romans mark the difference between Venus and Diana, as the Greeks do between
Aphrodite and Artemis? Look at the contrast
between Virgil and Homer ! "

T.—" Surely Virgil does not write much about
Diana ? "

G.—" He has the line :

'Tergeminamque Hecaten, tria virginis ora Dianæ.'

See, too, how Horace confounds Diana with Proserpine in the passage:

'Infernis neque enim tenebris Diana pudicum
Liberat Hippolytum.'"

I suggested that in this instance Horace seemed to me to refer to Diana, not as identical with Proserpine, but as the goddess whom Hippolytus especially worshipped. Mr. Gladstone frankly said that this was a new idea to him, but that he would think it over.

He supposed that Horace, though his Odes were Greek in form, was the best authority for the state of Roman society in classical times. But the discrepancies in his account are a puzzle. Sometimes he writes in glowing language; at other times he speaks of the state of society as hopelessly corrupt. Mr. Gladstone could not accept the common interpretation of

"O utinam nova
Incude diffingas retusum in
Massagetas Arabasque ferrum."

This he explained to mean: "Break up our corrupt civilisation, and remould us after the fashion of barbarous tribes." I demurred to this explanation; but, in support of it, I reminded him of the *Arva beata, etc.*, which seems to have partly suggested the passage in *Locksley Hall*, beginning—

"Ah, for some retreat
Deep in yonder shining Orient,"

Another passage which he thought wrongly interpreted is—

> "Nec fortuitum spernere cæspitem
> Leges sinebant."

G.—"I do not think there is any point in the rendering 'chance turf.' What would they do with it? Not build. Conington suggests that they might make their roofs of it. I know that they so construct their roofs in Iceland and elsewhere, where it is hard to get wood. But otherwise I do not think that they would make their roofs of turf alone. I think it refers to the enclosure of commons, and so it touches on a question which has lately been coming to the front."

I asked how he explained "spernere." He said that it meant "to disregard the laws which forbid the appropriation of the *ager publicus*." But he admitted that his view was not free from difficulty.

I said that we probably learn as much about Roman society from Juvenal, though his account must be taken as a caricature; and I added that, as Matthew Arnold says, we gather from Marcus Aurelius that there must have been a large portion of Italian life free from the corruption which Juvenal describes. Mr. Gladstone quite agreed.

We talked about Mr. Gladstone's Romanes Lecture. I told him that in that lecture he appeared to me to ignore the great progress in jurisprudence made by the Romans under the Empire; and that, on the other hand, he laid too great, or at any rate too exclusive, stress on their progress in arms. He replied by calling my attention to the military achievements of Belisarius and Narses. But I confess that he seemed to me to be ascribing to progress in the military art what was rather due to the military genius of a few individuals. I quoted what Maine, in his *Ancient Law*, said about the great development of jurisprudence under the Roman Empire.

G.—" I give way on this point to the authority of such an expert as Maine. But in the lecture I was trying to insist that life had departed from the Roman civilisation. What remarkable men did that civilisation produce ? "

I mentioned Claudian.

G.—" Yes, but that is not saying much. I think that the decline of paganism has never been sufficiently explained. Gibbon's account is too one-sided. I wish it could have been discussed by such a writer as Hallam." He spoke in praise of Beugnot's *Décadence du Paganisme en Occident*. Beugnot also wrote a *Décadence en Orient*, but it was not so good. The former book was *Couronnée par l'Académie française* in 1826. "This is not much of a distinction now, but it was then." He spoke of the long resistance offered by Paganism to Christianity.

G.—" Probably many of the ' pagani ' were devout pagans, and there seem to have been also some devout pagans among the educated classes. But these latter were few; and Beugnot traces the different causes, such as historical and family traditions, and more interested motives, which prolonged the life of dying Paganism."

T.—" Besides the believers in Paganism, were there not many who bore to Paganism the same sort of relation that Matthew Arnold bore to Christianity? I refer to such men as Marcus Aurelius, who thought it important that the masses should have a religion, and who held that the best religion for them was the religion of the State. Such men would probably have wished to purify the national religion of some of its coarser elements; but, in general, they would be afraid, to use Bright's metaphor, of tinkering an old institution."

G.—" Very likely there were a good number of these; and the position of Marcus Aurelius may in some respects have been like that of Matthew Arnold. But Marcus Aurelius did not write about his religion in the patronising way in which Matthew Arnold writes about Christianity. I know nothing that jars me more than the tone he takes."

T.—" Was not that partly the peculiar manner of the man?"

G.—" It may have been; but I often wish that he would make his bow and walk on the other side. To come back to my Romanes Lecture: my object was to combat Pattison's statement that the extinction of the Pagan civilisation by the Church was a great calamity."

T.—" I suspect that Pattison, if pressed, would have explained his words to mean that it is deplorable that human nature is such a poor thing that it cannot maintain its civilisation on a rational and progressive footing, and that it is forced from time to time to fall back on supernaturalism."

January 29th, 1894.—I dined with Mr. Gladstone. He expressed great interest in the customs of the Basques, and in the unsolved riddle of the origin of their race and language. Had not Scaliger satirically exclaimed: "*The Basques say that they understand one another, but they lie!*" Mr. Gladstone seemed especially taken with the popular myth explanatory of the high morality common among them: "*The Devil took seven years trying to learn Basque, and at last gave it up as a bad job.*" A saying of Basque origin seemed equally quaint, though in a different fashion: "Our Lord promised to give St. Peter a horse if he would repeat the Lord's Prayer without pause or interpolation. Whereupon St. Peter began: '*Pater noster qui es in cœlis*'— And, Lord, will he have a saddle?"

Mr. Gladstone had been reading a lecture on the sanitary rules followed by the Jews. I said that I had been told that in England they were less long-lived than Christians. His impression was the other way. He said that they had a special immunity from tubercular disease. Reference was made to a *quondam* Professor whose too catholic antipathies were especially directed against the Jewish race and modern Liberals; and one of the party reported that this Ishmael, on being told that the Jews had a remarkable immunity from cholera, drily exclaimed,

"That is the worst thing I have heard of the cholera!"

G. (*smiling*)—"He hates the Jews as much as he hates me." The genial tone of this remark may serve to show that Mr. Gladstone was not as abnormally sensitive to adverse criticism as he was often said to be.

He did not take the same high view that many take of the old Hebrew literature, regarded merely as literature. He had been struck by a statement of Professor Max Müller to the effect that the Jewish intellect made a sudden start after being brought in contact with the Aryan intellect. (Surely Isaiah was an exception.) He did not think much of the old biblical heroes, except Moses. I hinted at a scepticism about Moses being a real person. He said that he thought that, if there had been no historical Moses, the Hebrew imagination would not have been equal to the task of creating one. And then he went off to his favourite subject.

G.—"Those who think it too great a miracle that there should have been a Homer who wrote both the *Iliad* and the *Odyssey*, are substituting for it a miracle yet greater and yet harder of belief."

I remarked that, if the word ἀμύμων really means "blameless," it seems very odd that in the beginning of the *Odyssey* this epithet is applied to Ægisthus. He replied that "blameless" is a very inadequate rendering of the word. It may sometimes mean this; but sometimes also it connotes high birth; "just as we apply the word 'illustrious' to princes—

to such princes as the sons of George III. There are other expressions in Homer which we were taught to translate either incorrectly or in too narrow a sense; for instance, at Eton, Edward Coleridge insisted on our translating ἄναξ ἀνδρῶν, 'king of men.'"

I asked Mr. Gladstone why he had not ranked *Rob Roy* with those novels of Walter Scott which he placed in the first rank. He thought that *Rob Roy* and *Guy Mannering* ran them very hard. He was surprised when I mentioned that Lowe had ranked *St. Ronan's Well* with the *Bride of Lammermoor*. He agreed with me that this was an instance of the peculiar limitation which is so often found in men of strong individuality. I asked whether he admired Miss Austen much.

G.—"Certainly. But I am not so enthusiastic about her as some people are. An old friend of mine, Rio (he is long since dead), complained that Macaulay 'can neither dive nor soar.' This is true of Jane Austen. Someone said of Randolph Churchill (it was only true of him in his earlier days), that 'he was a first-rate actor in a third-rate piece.' This also might be said of Miss Austen."

T.—"Walter Scott has spoken of himself as successful in the bow-wow strain, while Miss Austen excelled in the representation of everyday life."

G.—"That is Walter Scott's modest way of putting things. He was generosity itself. In all those volumes of his there is a complete absence of self-laudation. After all, Miss Austen was *parochial,* while Scott was *world-historical—Welt-historisch,* as the Germans would say."

I complained that some of Miss Austen's characters seemed to me wooden; they contrast in that way with some of Miss Ferrier's.

G.—" Which of Miss Ferrier's have you read ? "

T.—" *Marriage.*"

G.—" You should read her *Inheritance.* It is far her best. She had the great advantage of writing in the interval between the earlier and the later school of novelists."

Mr. Gladstone ranked Disraeli as the greatest master of parliamentary wit that had ever been. He looked upon his character as a great mystery, and it pained him to feel that the mystery will never be solved. He quoted Bright's remark on the representation of minorities: " If the member for a minority dies, will the minority have the power of electing his successor ? " This Mr. Gladstone thought a perfectly fair criticism, well expressed. He said that Disraeli disliked the idea of representation of minorities; but he introduced it into his Reform Bill as a sop to political *doctrinaires.* Afterwards, when the House of Lords amended his Reform Bill and made it practically a nominal measure, Disraeli threw out all their amendments with the exception of this one, which, though he disliked it, he thought comparatively unimportant. Mr. Gladstone thought that the wittiest thing which Bright ever said was when he spoke of the party which formed the Cave of Adullam as being like a Skye terrier: "it was so covered with hair that you could not tell its head from its tail."[1] The leading members of the Cave were Lowe and Horsman, the latter of whom Mr. Gladstone described as "a mere windbag." He added that Bright meant to imply that both these members uttered such platitudes that those of Lowe were on a par with those of Horsman. Mr. Gladstone spoke of Lowe's inability to defend himself.

G.—"The power of self-defence is implanted in the meanest of all creatures (I don't know whether it exists in rabbits). But at any rate it was absent in Lowe. He, who had attacked our Reform Bill so powerfully, was quite helpless when such an inferior man as —— attacked him. Dizzy quite cut him to pieces. In one way this told morally in his favour. A member of a Government is bound to defend his colleagues as much as himself; and, as Lowe did not defend his colleagues, it told in his favour that he also did not defend himself."

The wittiest thing that Mr. Gladstone ever heard

[1] It is well known that the christening of the party as "The Cave of Adullam" was also due to Bright; but it is less well known that, in making the comparison, he was in a manner anticipated by Mr. Gladstone's favourite novelist: "The Baron of Bradwardine, being asked what he thought of these recruits, took a long pinch of snuff, and answered drily, that he could not but have an excellent opinion of them, since they resembled precisely the followers who attached themselves to the good King David at the cave of Adullam ; *videlicet,* everyone that was in distress, everyone that was in debt, and everyone that was discontented, which the Vulgate renders *bitter of soul.*"

in Parliament was a retort of Lord John Russell.
Sir Francis Burdett had been a strong Radical;
and, as is well known, he got into trouble about
it. After some years, he became a Conservative.
Mr. Gladstone doubted whether his inconsistency
was as great as it seemed to be. But at any rate it
brought him into opposition with his old colleagues.
He made a rather violent speech, in which he said
there was nothing he hated so much as the " cant of
patriotism." Lord John Russell got up and said
that, for himself, there was one thing that he hated
worse, and that was " the *recant* of patriotism."

The best thing said in Parliament in this century
was, Mr. Gladstone thought, a sentence of Canning.
Pitt had been a Free Trader; but in his later life he
took a line which naturally made the Tories claim
him as a Protectionist. Canning was thoroughly
devoted to his old master, and used to say that his
allegiance was with Pitt in his tomb. He said of
those Protectionists who appealed to the authority
of Pitt: " They are like those savages who pay
no honour to the sun when he is in his meridian
splendour, but who, when he is under a momentary
eclipse, come forth with cymbals and dances to adore
him." [1]

[1] A few days later Mr. Gladstone, at my request, most kindly
repeated his version of Canning's metaphor, and then let me repeat
it to him ; so that my account of that version is certainly correct.
It differs slightly from the ordinary version, which is as follows :
"Such perverse worship is like the idolatry of barbarous nations,
who can see the noonday splendour of the sun without emotion, but,
when he is in eclipse, come forward with their hymns and cymbals

8

Canning was an adept in such rhetorical out-bursts. Some forty years ago, I heard an old gentleman, in a speech at an agricultural dinner, quote with great admiration the following sentence which in his youth he had heard from Canning's own lips:—"The same sun which lighted Lord Wellington into Madrid and which grew pale at the conflagration of Moscow, has yielded us the most luxuriant harvest that has ever blessed mankind." Surely this rhetoric is overstrained. If it is not mere verbiage, it implies that the stars in their courses had fought against Napoleon; and it seems to postulate such a belief in the anthropomorphic and anthropocentric—I had almost said Anglo-centric—government of the physical world as is in nowise warranted by science.

I reminded Mr. Gladstone of the saying of Burke about Warren Hastings, which Macaulay has thus recorded: "It was said that at Benares, the very place at which the acts set forth in the first article of impeachment had been committed, the natives had erected a temple to Hastings; and this story excited a strong sensation in England. Burke's observations on the apotheosis were admirable. He saw no reason for astonishment, he said, in the incident which had been represented as so striking. He knew something of the mythology of the Brah-

to adore him." Mr. Gladstone's version, however, delivered as it was in a voice far more sonorous and rhetorical than was his wont in conversation, seems to me interesting and characteristic ; it is, as it were, Canning Gladstonized.

mins. He knew that, as they worshipped some gods from love, so they worshipped others from fear. He knew that they erected shrines, not only to the benignant deities of light and plenty, but also to the fiends who preside over small-pox and murder. Nor did he at all dispute the claim of Mr. Hastings to be admitted into such a Pantheon."

G.—"Did Burke say that on the spur of the moment?"

T.—"I do not know; but probably he did not."

G.—"That makes all the difference. If I am asked who is the greatest speaker that I have known in Parliament, I answer that it depends on what you mean by a great speaker. No one was equal to Bright when he had time to prepare a subject. But he was not strong as a debater, though I once remember his being very successful in debate. I think it was about Ireland; but I am not sure. I once had an odd experience. It was found convenient that I, as leader of the party, should make a speech from Bright's notes. I will mention another small experience that I had. Ayrton was often a very troublesome opponent in debate. I remember once that at three o'clock in the morning he was going to attack me. I saw him go out of the House to eat an orange, and knew *that* probably meant an hour's speech. This was too much, and I beat a prudent retreat. As you take an interest in these Parliamentary reminiscences, I will give you another. The Conservatives appointed Lord Glenelg to a high official position. He was thoroughly honourable, but was supposed to be inefficient, and had a way of falling asleep during debates. In the course of a very exciting debate, Brougham in the House of Lords expressed regret that he and his party had deprived the noble Lord of so many sleepless days. I reminded Brougham of this afterwards, and was glad to find that he had quite forgotten it. It showed that his wit was so abundant that he could afford to forget particular instances of it."

T.—"In fact, he was, in Tennyson's phrase, 'Like wealthy men who care not how they give.'"

I asked Mr. Gladstone about Peel; he did not seem to have left on record many witty sayings.

G.—"No; Peel was not a phrase-maker, like Disraeli or Bright. There were two things especially conspicuous about him. One was his overmastering sense of public duty; this never deserted him. The other thing was his sense of measure. He had generally an exact sense of the proportion between one Bill, and the general policy of the Government; also of the proportion between the different parts of the same Bill; and of the relation in which the leaders of his party stood to their followers. What I mean by this sense of measure will be understood if I give an instance in which such tact was conspicuously wanting. Shortly (I think) after the Reform Bill, the Conservative leaders had got the party into a state of what seemed hopeless confusion. So much so that one

night they were preparing to send in their resignation. Fortunately for them, Lord Grey made an
attack on the party as a whole. This so irritated
the followers that they rallied under their leaders,
and the party held its ground."

I asked Mr. Gladstone whether Peel was not very
unsociable in private life. An old M.P. once told me
that, when he dined with Peel, Peel used to beset
him with questions, and to give out nothing in
return.

G.—"Quite right too. If Peel had to do with
someone from whom useful information could be
got, he was quite right to try and get it. If he was
wanting in sociability, the reason was that his mind
was too full of the public interest to be able to
occupy itself with smaller matters."

T.—"But surely he might have given out something on non-political matters; for example, on
literature or history."

G.—"He sometimes did. I remember his praising to me Hallam as a historian. Also, I heard
him express a low opinion of Fox. So far as
Fox's private character is concerned, Peel may
have been right; but, as a public man, Fox had
certainly a remarkable power of grasping general
principles."

At first these examples of Peel's communicativeness
seemed to me conspicuous by their slightness; but I
afterwards reflected that, according to Professor
Goldwin Smith, " For personal recollections twenty-
three years are Lethe "; and that twice that interval

divided us from the point of time to which Mr. Gladstone was reaching back.

Mr. Gladstone thought that there was a certain resemblance between Rome under Augustus and France under Louis Napoleon. I called attention to the resemblance between the two Cæsars in their relation to one another, and the two Napoleons.

G.—" Yes. The resemblance is remarkable in many ways; though Augustus was much wiser in his generation than Louis Napoleon."

T.—" Was not Louis Napoleon wise in his generation during the earlier part of his career ? "

G.—" Certainly not from the time of the Mexican expedition. But what I am insisting on as a point of resemblance between the two despots is that, while Louis Napoleon put down freedom of speech and of writing in general, he allowed a certain freedom to men of letters who were not likely to influence the public. And I suspect it was the same sort of thing with Augustus. So long as Horace made a low bow to the established Government, he was allowed in an indirect way to show his sympathy with his old comrades of Philippi."

T.—" In the one stanza, *Olim Philippos*, there are two phrases which the admirers of Horace try to explain away. *Turpe solum tetigere mento*, and *relicta non bene parmula*. It is said that no Roman soldier would have made the latter admission. But surely he meant that he had been so insignificant an enemy, that the conquerors could afford to overlook his youthful folly."

G.—"That is what I meant by the low bow. I believe that Louis Napoleon was often indulgent to Orleanist men of letters who veiled their meaning."

T.—"Did you personally see enough of Louis Napoleon to form an impression of his ability?"

G.—"No. I dined with him in the Tuileries. But he was most of the time cross-questioning me about English finance." (He said this with a smile which seemed to mean, *If Louis Napoleon thus cross-examined, why should not Peel?*) "The conversation was in English, which he spoke very well. I saw him again during his exile. But I found him then a broken man, and could not judge of his ability."

We spoke about Froude, and the question was raised whether, after all, it had been a mistake to confer on him the Professorship of History. Was not such a style as Froude's a supreme merit in a Professor? His facts might be often inaccurate; but they were certainly far less so than the facts introduced into Scott's novels; and yet Scott's novels are valued as carrying a picturesque conception of the past into quarters where otherwise there would be no conception of it at all. Scott's Richard I. is more of a permanent possession, more of a living person, than Hume's. Is it not possible that, in like manner, some of Froude's historical portraits will survive Freeman's?

Mr. Gladstone spoke severely of the peculiar bias shown by Froude with regard to Henry VIII. We got on the charm of Froude's diction as contrasted with Grote's, and I mentioned the substance of Charles Austin's comment on Grote, which is thus reported in *Safe Studies*: "He feared that the *History of Greece* lost much of its value through the attempt to whitewash Cleon and the other demagogues. He also regretted that Mr. Grote had bestowed so little pains on his style; an inattention which seemed to Mr. Austin all the more strange as the historian was keenly alive to the grace and charm of the classical writings. He was afraid that, in consequence of these two defects, the history of Greece still remained to be written."

Mr. Gladstone said that he had heard Grote find fault with the English of John Mill. I said that I thought that Grote may have been very particular in avoiding slipshod sentences.

G.—"But are there any such sentences in Mill?"

T.—"I should think very few; but I remember seeing one or two quoted by Professor Hodgson in his *Errors in the Use of English.*"

Mr. Gladstone did not seem to have heard of this book. I mentioned that its author had marshalled a long array of blunders from various writers, great and small; and I told Mr. Gladstone of two instances given by Hodgson of the wrong collocation of words:—"Erected to the memory of John Phillips accidentally shot as a mark of affection by his brother;" and "A piano for sale by a lady about to cross the Channel in an oak case with carved legs." Mr. Gladstone seemed much amused by these examples. In reference to the general question, he thought that a sentence ought not to bear more than one construction, and he quoted the familiar *Aio te, Æacide, Romanos vincere posse.*

Mr. Gladstone spoke playfully of a lady as his step-great-niece; and asked what I made of such a relation. I said in a like tone that, Queen Charlotte having been godmother of my mother-in-law, I have sometimes spoken of George III. as my step-god-grand-father-in-law.

G. (with a smile).—"I was going to say that I wished you a better step-god—I forget the rest;—but I draw a distinction. George III. in his private character shows to advantage when compared with Charles II. or George II. But, if George III. had succeeded in repressing freedom and parliamentary government, we should have had a Revolution, not probably so bad as the French, but resembling it in kind. From such a catastrophe we were preserved by that unworthy representative of good principles, Wilkes."

We referred to Macaulay's praise of William III., and to his speaking less severely of William's private faults than of those of James II.

G.—"Of course it was as a public man that Macaulay praised William; but I have no doubt that Macaulay's bias in favour of William extended to everything about him."

While admiring many points in Miss Cholmondeley's *Diana Tempest,* Mr. Gladstone found fault with that clever novel, first, because he thought that a novel with an abnormal plot requires very exceptional skill; and, secondly, because the authoress throws satire broadcast on the clergy and other representatives of tradition. He did not object to *Robert Elsmere* on this ground, because the orthodox Catherine is represented as narrow perhaps, but on the whole an ideal character.

We spoke of the Revised Translation of the Bible. He said that he had advised the translators (or some of them) to bring out, at an early stage, a few specimens of their work and to let the critics say their say about them. To anyone versed in the usages of the House of Commons such an expedient would not seem unnatural. But the translators utterly refused to suffer their unfinished work to be blown on by the *popularis aura* of inexperts: "They laughed me to scorn; and the result has been that the Revised Version died almost at its birth."

I think it was on this occasion that Mr. Gladstone made a remark to me which has been treasured up in my memory. Taking my arm as we left the dining-room, he said, "Your memory makes you formidable; but you are so good-natured that one does not feel afraid of you." At first the word "afraid" employed by the great Statesman fairly took my breath away; I felt disposed to say, "Quid enim contendat hirundo Cycnis?" But, on second thoughts, I interpreted the hyperbolical compliment to mean, "I am sure that, if you Boswellize me, you will set down nought in malice." In other words, he more than suspected that I was taking notes of our conversations. It is as throwing light on this point that his observation seemed to me worth recording.

January 13*th*, 1896.—Mr. and Mrs. Gladstone and Mrs. Drew dined with us.

He remarked on our being in the same rooms as before.

T.—"You see I have strong Conservative instincts."

G.—"So have I. In all matters of custom and tradition, even the Tories look upon me as the chief Conservative that is."

T.—"Two years ago a Conservative M.P. spoke of you as the strongest Conservative influence in Parliament. This being so, I wondered why, in the interests of Conservatism, he did not join your party."

Mr. Gladstone smiled and seemed pleased.

I note, in passing, that my Conservative friend probably regarded Mr. Gladstone as the best controller and moderator of the political changes which have become inevitable; insomuch that the English Government under his guidance might be compared to the Athenian Government under the guidance of Pericles: "it was nominally a democracy, but in reality the supremacy of the first citizen" (λόγῳ μὲν δημοκρατία ἔργῳ δὲ ὑπὸ τοῦ πρώτου ἀνδρὸς ἄρχη).

He spoke with high praise of Purcell's *Life of Manning.* He said it was the "history of a soul and the dividing of bone and marrow." He had read no biography for some time " which showed so much impartiality and insight."   I asked him what he thought of Manning as an orator.   He said that he had heard some striking sermons of Manning's while Manning was still in the Church of England. He evidently thought much more highly of Newman as a master of English ; but he called Manning " a great Ecclesiastical Statesman."   I asked him about Cardinal Vaughan.

G.—" Oh, he is an infinitely smaller man.   I am reminded of Canning's lines." [1]

This suggested the appointment of Alfred Austin as successor to Alfred Tennyson.

T.—" Was it not a pity appointing a new laureate ? The office is now altogether something of an ana-chronism ; why could it not have a grand euthanasia in Tennyson ? "

G.—" At any rate I should have waited until some-one of Tennyson's calibre had turned up.   I felt a special difficulty in recommending a successor to Tennyson, because by far the greatest of our English poets is practically out of the running."

He went on to give reasons for this latter opinion, and spoke of some lines in which the great living poet to whom he referred had touched on the death of the late Czar.   I expressed surprise that the difficulty about Mr. William Morris' political opinions could not be got over.

---

[1] " Pitt is to Addington
As London to Paddington."

G.—"Would you place him as a poet anywhere near Swinburne?"

T.—"The two are so unlike that they can hardly be compared. But I confess that I admire much of the *Earthly Paradise* and of *The Life and Death of Jason.*"

I expressed surprise at the extremely high praise which Matthew Arnold and others bestow on Wordsworth. Mr. Gladstone replied that he was also surprised; but he added that he had heard that the late Sir Francis Doyle, whose critical faculty he valued highly, took the same view as Matthew Arnold. Neither Mr. Gladstone nor I could understand why Matthew Arnold ranked Wordsworth so much above Tennyson. I quoted single lines of Wordsworth which Matthew Arnold praised highly. Matthew Arnold seemed to regard the line—

"Will no one tell me what she sings?"

and the line—

"And never lifted up a single stone,"

as so admirable in themselves that, even when severed from their context, they furnish a sort of touchstone which may help us to discriminate between good poetry and bad. Would Dr. Arnold have thought so highly of either of these lines if they had been written by a Rugby boy?

I added that Matthew Arnold speaks contemptuously of Macaulay's *Lays.*

G.—"I admire the *Lays* very much. *They will live.*"

I called Mr. Gladstone's attention to the extraordinary passage in which Matthew Arnold hazards the opinion that Shelley's letters may outlive his poems. Mr. Gladstone seemed to agree with me that criticisms of this kind tend to shake one's faith in the critic's judgment.

I asked Mr. Gladstone what he thought of Macaulay as a speaker. He gave an account of two famous speeches of Macaulay's and of the effect that they produced; but he admitted that it was only on very rare occasions that Macaulay achieved such results.

I asked him whether he thought Bright the finest speaker he had ever heard in Parliament.

G.—"That is very hard to answer. There is so much that goes to make a great orator. But I will say that there were certain passages in Bright's speeches which I never heard equalled."

T.—"Had not these been carefully prepared?"

G.—"They were said to be."

T.—"Was Peel a great orator?"

G.—"Not at all in the same way."

Mr. Gladstone seemed to think that Peel's reputation as a statesman stands somewhat too high. He did not remember to have read Mr. Thursfield's *Life of Peel*. But he had spoken to the eminent author about Sir Robert; and he expected that the book would exactly represent his own views.

G.—"The great virtue of Peel was that he had

such an enormous conscience.   Conscience, they say,
is a very expensive thing to keep.   Peel certainly
kept one."

T.—" But you will remember that Peel was compared (I think by Disraeli) to the Turkish admiral
who treacherously steered the fleet under his command into the enemy's harbour; and, exaggeration
apart, I suppose you would say that, on the two great
occasions of Catholic Emancipation and Free Trade,
other men laboured and he entered into their labours."

G.—" Yes.   But, when he had finally made up
his mind, he stuck to it unflinchingly.   His great
failure was in regard to Ireland.   He thought that
he could *cobble up* the Irish difficulty by endow-
ing Maynooth and establishing what the strong
Protestants call godless Colleges.   In one instance
he, from most conscientious motives, did the Irish
a great injury.   He passed the Encumbered Estates
Act.   It is fair to say that, when the cottiers improved their land, the old landlords did not tread
on the heels of the improvement.   But, after the
passing of Peel's Act, when any land came to be
sold, the buyer naturally wanted to get the full
value of his money; and so the poor tenant lost all
the value of his improvement.   One thing may
amuse you.   In the new *National Biography* only
fifteen pages are given to Peel, and twenty pages to
Parnell."

T.—" You once told me that Parnell's speeches
reminded you of Lord Palmerston's in their way of
expressing exactly what the speaker meant to say.

But of course you would call Parnell a pigmy compared with Lord Palmerston."

G.—"I should not call him anything of the sort. He had statesmanlike qualities; and I found him a wonderfully good man to do business with [1] . . .

T.—"What sort of a place, then, would you assign to Lord Palmerston?"

G.—"Taking our former standard of measurement, I should say that, if Peel has fifteen pages of the *Biography*, Palmerston should have ten or twelve. Palmerston had two admirable qualities. He had an intense love of Constitutional freedom everywhere; and he had a profound hatred of negro slavery. One signal service he rendered to Ireland. He appointed the 'Devon Commission,' which collected facts proving the Irish to be the most oppressed, the most miserable and the most patient population in Europe. But he did not make any practical use of this knowledge. I should not ascribe to him the overpowering conscientiousness which I ascribe to Peel."

I quoted as accurately as I could the passage in Bacon's essay "Of Goodness, and Goodness of Nature," in which, after describing certain not very benevolent or trustworthy characters, he says of them: "Such dispositions are the very errors of human nature; and yet they are the fittest timber to make great politicks of; like to knee timber, that is good for ships that are ordained to be

---

[1] A phrase is here omitted which, I am assured, did not express Mr. Gladstone's deliberate opinion.

tossed, but not for building houses that shall stand firm." I suggested that in this passage absolute honesty is recommended to ordinary men, but that a certain amount of dissimulation is conceded to statesmen. Does not this recall Tacitus's remark on Galba's refusal to temporise? To that high standard, he tells us, *jam non pares sumus.*

G.—"It is only with great hesitation that I should differ from anything that Bacon says in those *Essays* of his. But surely knee timber is not a thing which bends as an unscrupulous man's conscience bends. It is chosen because it is in the shape best suited to ships."

T.—"I suppose that Bacon meant that it is naturally crooked, just as some men's consciences are naturally crooked."

G.—"Well, I should not say this of Palmerston's conscience. An illustration will best show the fault that I find with him. When the troubles were arising between Prussia and Denmark, Palmerston said that, if the Danes were attacked, they would not stand alone. They were attacked; they did stand alone; and Palmerston did not resign."

T.—"Of course, when he said that, he thought that the cause of Denmark would be warmly supported by England."

G.—"He had no business to think. There was an Eton master, named Heath, who had an odd sort of dry humour. When he was going to send a boy up to be flogged, and the boy began to make excuses, saying 'I thought so-and-so,' he used to

9

say, 'No boy has any business to think until he gets to the Upper Division.' And so Palmerston had no business to think until he had learnt what the country was prepared to do." [1]

Something was said about flogging in public schools; and I told the story of how Dr. Vaughan was once flogging a young nobleman, who, not being used to such rough treatment, presently got up and asked the headmaster how many more cuts he was going to give. Vaughan replied in his most mellifluous voice, "That is for me to decide, Lord F.; kneel down again." A lady told the story of an assistant master sending Keate a list of boys to be confirmed. Keate thought they were to be flogged, and flogged them accordingly. I called Mr. Gladstone's attention to the phrase he had used, " dry-humour," remarking that, according to the etymology, it would signify *dry-wetness*. Wishing to draw him out about wit and humour, I mentioned that Matthew Arnold says that Molière ought to be ranked with Shakespeare, Milton, and Goethe.

G.—"Does he indeed say that? I should not call Molière a poet."

T.—"I once expressed some surprise to our friend J—— M—— at so high a place being assigned to

---

[1] This may recall a passage in *The Rivals* :—

LYDIA.—"Madam, I thought you once "—

MRS. MALAPROP.—"You thought, Miss! I don't know any business you have to think at all—thought does not become a young woman."

Molière; but he agreed with Matthew Arnold. He said that Molière had written two plays, which fell only just below the greatest dramas of the world; and he also spoke very highly of *L'Avare*, and also praised the *Bourgeois Gentilhomme*."

G.—" Well, I suppose that the *Misanthrope* and the *Tartuffe* were the two great plays that he meant. I have been reading them lately, and I should call them both third-class plays. I once asked Döllinger whom he considered the two wittiest men that ever lived. He at once answered, ' Aristophanes and Shakespeare.' This is just what I should have said myself. I am very old now, and cannot hope to learn much more. But I do want to learn what the difference is, which people are so fond of talking about, between wit and humour."

I quoted Jowett's saying (*Memoir*, p. 32) that wit consists in a number of points, while humour is continuous.

G.—" I don't see how he would have applied that to individual cases. One of the best things ever said was the remark of Falstaff, who, being called on to pay for the satin which he had purchased, said that Bardolph should be his surety.[1] Was this wit or humour ? "

T.—" At any rate, there can be no doubt that most of Sydney Smith's good sayings were witty

---

[1] The reference is to *Henry IV.*, Part II. Act i. Scene 2. But I fail to detect in this scene any quotable passage which would not disappoint my readers, after the praise bestowed by Mr. Gladstone.

rather than humorous. Take the familiar example of the young lady who said to him, 'We want to bring this pea to perfection'; Sydney Smith, giving her his arm, replied, 'Let me bring perfection to the pea.'"

G.—"Yes, that was wit. By the way, I am told that one of the Pollocks was the author of a saying which I had always supposed to be by Sydney Smith—the saying addressed to the child who tried to please the tortoise by stroking its shell: 'You might as well stroke the Dome of St. Paul's to please the Dean and Chapter.' The little *gamins* sometimes say very good things. Someone who applied to us for a clerkship told us that he had already applied to become a clerk to an undertaker in Fetter Lane—not a very lively occupation. But what can have been his feelings when, on going to the office, he found two hundred other applicants? But the unkindest cut of all was when he saw two small *gamins* pointing at them, and saying, 'Look at all those clerks; they are going there to be measured for their coffins.' I will give you another instance. A very tall friend of mine was staring up at the Obelisk. He heard one of the *gamins* say, 'If you were to lie on the ground, you would be half-way home.'"

T.—"I know a case of a very tall, gaunt, and plain English lady in Spain, to whom a rude little Spanish boy said, 'You are as long and as ugly as a lawsuit.'"

May not, I am tempted to ask, the difference

between wit and humour be illustrated by Sydney Smith's definition of wit? "The feeling of wit," he says, "is occasioned by those relations of ideas which excite surprise, and surprise alone." Now, it is manifest that the limitation contained in this last clause would not be required in a definition of humour. Nay, it represents the very opposite of what is required in such a definition. The emotional quality which (according to Sydney Smith) wit lacks, all humour must possess. Why, then, should not humour be defined as *Wit touched by emotion*?

The conversation drifted to English literature.

T.—" I find it hard to think that Carlyle's extreme popularity will last very long."

G. (smiling)—" I find it hard to be impartial; for Carlyle did not at all like me."

T.—" Also, he did not at all like Disraeli, at least before Disraeli offered him a knighthood."

G.—" Yes, I know that he did not like Dizzy; but, with regard to myself, the hard thing was that I had a long, interesting, and, as it seemed to me, amicable conversation with him at Mentone; and then, to my amazement, I found, when Froude's life of him came out, this very conversation is mentioned in it, and I am described as utterly contemptible and impermeable to new ideas. I don't look upon Carlyle as a philosopher. Tennyson once said to me a very good thing about him. He said, ' Carlyle is a poet, to whom Nature has denied the faculty of verse.' "

T.—" This reminds me of what Tennyson said

to a friend of mine about Walt Whitman. He said,
'The first requisite of a singer is that he should
sing. Walt Whitman has not this requisite; let
him speak in prose.'"

G.—"Does not this seem rather inconsistent with
what he said to me?"

T.—"I think not. He seemingly regarded both
Carlyle and Walt Whitman as poetical torsos, as
poets without the faculty of verse. This being so,
he blamed Walt Whitman for attempting verse.
He would doubtless have commended Carlyle for
never (or hardly ever) attempting it."

G.—"Are you a great admirer of Carlyle?"

T.—"At Harrow I became a great admirer of
Macaulay's directness and plainness, and I often
wish that Carlyle would not write Carlylese."

G. (smiling)—"I suppose that it is hardly possible
for the same man to be a great admirer both of
Macaulay and of Carlyle."

The conversation passed on to politics.

T.—"I don't want to embark on too wide a
subject; but I am tempted to ask in the words of
Jehoram, 'Is it peace, Jehu?' In other words,
are you at all afraid of war, especially with
Germany?"

G.—"Not in the least."

T.—"Are you not afraid of our small army being
attacked by their huge army?"

G.—"How are they to cross the Channel without
ships? *They would get very wet!*"

Mrs. T.—"Might they not use a great number

of the German Lloyd steamers to transport their army ? ”

G.—“ We should have twenty ships to their one.”

T.—“ I suppose that some English companies might be induced to supply them with ships and arms.”

G.—“ Oh yes. For filthy lucre they would supply arms to the rebel angels against Heaven.”

T.—“ This reminds me of the case of the *Alabama.*”

G.—“ The case of the *Alabama* is a very difficult and complicated one.”

T.—“ I suppose that you consider the award was extravagantly high.”

G.—“ It was enormous.”

He went on to mention, if I understood him rightly, a case in which we were mulcted of a large sum through the act of one of our colonies.

T.—“ What a strong view Froude takes in *Oceana* about the importance of colonies to the Mother Country !”

G.—“ What reason does he give ? ”

T.—“ I think he says that in England the race tends to become enfeebled through being crowded into large towns. He wishes more and more emigrants to be sent off to Australia and the other colonies, so that they or their posterity may return with recruited vigour to do service in England.”

G.—“ Does he propose bringing another Australia into being ? The conditions which he seems to have desired exist already, and I cannot see how he expected to improve them. No, I have always maintained that we are bound by ties of honour and conscience to our colonies. But the idea that the colonies add to the strength of the mother country appears to me to be as dark a superstition as any that existed in the Middle Ages."

It may not be amiss to compare this with a remark made in conversation many years ago by the late editor of the *Times* (Mr. Chenery) in regard to the colonies: " They are not feeders, but suckers."

In justice to Froude, I feel bound to say that I understand his contention to be that the colonies must be made to feel that the mother country really regards them as her children, and that she opens her doors to them, and is willing (in Academic phrase) to grant to those who distinguish themselves an *ad eundem* degree on her own soil; and that, this being clearly understood, the tie between mother country and colonies will gradually become closer, especially as quickened locomotion cuts short distance.

Later on, when Mr. Gladstone and I were left alone, he called my attention to the question raised in my *Memoir of Jowett* as to whether Socrates had much sense of sin.

T.—" Do you remember the passage at the end of the *Republic* where Socrates speaks of the tremendous and seemingly everlasting punishments which await tyrants in the other world? Does this not show that he had a strong sense of the heinousness of their sins?"

G.—" I do not doubt that Socrates felt strongly

the obligation of his moral code. But he regarded vice and crimes as offences against the social order, rather than as infractions of a law given by God. Of sin, in the latter sense, I think that there is no trace in Plato; and I am confident that there is none in Aristotle. Even the moral code of the Greeks in the time of Socrates was so elastic as to press very gently on the vice mentioned in the *Symposium.*"

T.—"It is certainly strange that there is nothing about that vice in Homer."

G.—"Yes; Homer had some remains of the sense of sin in his *ἀτασθαλίη.* But among the Greeks this sense of sin almost died out with Homer."

I recalled the declaration of Æschylus, which gathers solemnity from its very vagueness, and to which no translation can do justice—the half indignant, half incredulous declaration or admission that "someone denied" that the gods take any heed of mortals; and I asked whether Æschylus had not a deep sense, if not of sin, at any rate of the appalling seriousness of human life.

G.—"Yes, there are some remains of the sense of sin in Æschylus. In Homer the Eumenides are passionless beings dispensing impartial justice. In later times they are Furies inflamed by the worst passions. Take, for example, the phrase: *Atra flagellum Tisiphone quatit exultans.* In Æschylus you have both conceptions together."

I could not agree with him in thinking the Homeric gods by any means models of virtue. An example is furnished by the fight of the gods, and the attitude taken by the Supreme Father—

> " Jove as his sport the dreadful scene descries,
> And views contending gods with careless eyes."

In this couplet, it should be added, Pope has hardly done justice to the frank and refreshing brutality of the original, where the spiteful amusement of the Deity seems to be taken as a matter of course—

> " ἐγέλασσε δέ οἱ φίλον ἦτορ
> γηθοσύνη ὅθ' ὁρᾶτο θεοὺς ἔριδι συνίοντας."

May not, after all, this divine or diabolic mirth have been flavoured with a Chauvinistic ingredient—with the sweet but unwholesome condiment of *Dividantur et imperabo*?

Mr. Gladstone went on to say that, among the Hebrews in the time of Christ, the belief in the heinousness of sin had struck as deep root as the belief in the Unity of God; Christ himself did not insist on it, because He knew that His hearers did not dispute it.

On the general question I offered this comment: "I quite feel that the word 'sin,' in the theological sense, implies the infraction of a divine law. But is not this word, like some other theological terms (such as inspiration), gradually modifying its meaning? The distinction that we now want to mark, is the distinction between persons who have, and persons who have not, a strong capacity for righteous indignation. This capacity is not always coincident with a sense of sin (strictly so called). Rabelais, Montaigne, Shakespeare, Molière, and La

Fontaine probably believed—they certainly professed
to believe—in the delivery of the law from Sinai.
On the other hand, Voltaire, the two Mills, Mr.
Francis Newman and Mr. John Morley have rejected
that belief; and yet, strange to say, the capacity for
righteous indignation is far stronger in them than
in the earlier writers whom I have named; and
therefore, I should say that, in the modern accepta-
tion of the term, they have a stronger sense of the
heinousness of sin."

In connection with this subject I called Mr.
Gladstone's attention to a tremendous passage in
Newman's *Apologia*. "The Catholic Church holds
it better for the sun and moon to drop from heaven,
for the earth to fail, and for all the many millions
on it to die of starvation in extremest agony, as far
as temporal affliction goes, than that one soul, I will
not say, should be lost, but should commit one venial
sin, should tell one wilful untruth, or should steal
one poor farthing without excuse." Commenting on
this extract, I admitted that Newman's view might
be defended by very plausible arguments; but I
could not forbear testing it by a homely example.
Suppose that a boy, from sheer love of mischief, told
his parents falsely that his sister had been drowned.
On discovering the falsehood, the parents would
doubtless punish the boy well; but in their hearts
they would rejoice. In other words, they would
prefer that a small sin should have been committed,
rather than that a calamity should occur which
would be as dust in the balance when compared

with the calamity imagined by Newman. Would not even Newman himself have sympathised with such parents in their sense of relief ? Mr. Gladstone made no comment on what I urged, probably thinking that the interval between our respective standpoints was too wide to be bridged over by argument. But he helped on the discussion in another way. He gave me the extract (having himself most kindly copied it out) from Sir Henry Taylor's *Correspondence*, which he had mentioned to me in a former conversation as ascribing to Walter Scott a somewhat blunted capacity for moral indignation. The passage occurs in a letter:—" The defect which you mention is attributable to the defect of moral force in Scott's character; invariable candour and moderation in judging men is generally accompanied by such a defect. Scott seems to be always disposed to approve of rectitude of conduct, and to acquiesce in the general rules of morality, but without any instinctive or unconquerable aversion from vice— witness his friendship for Byron. Power of the imagination in conceiving and depicting strongly a great variety of characters seems scarcely compatible with a strong individuality of character in the person possessing that power. It is some simple, headstrong qualities which make a strong character. Universality of opinions, and especially of sympathies, the one generally arising out of extended knowledge, the other out of the poetic sensibilities, are compatible enough with the power of conceiving a strong character, but not with that of *being* it."

Mr. Gladstone added this comment: "Scott is one of my idols; but I cannot deny that there is force and depth in Taylor's doctrine. It is probably the only hard thing that can be, and has to be, said of Scott with truth. With this drawback, he was a great benefactor to mankind."

I could not forbear replying, "I own that Taylor seems to me hard on Scott. I cannot ascribe moral weakness to one who underwent such sacrifices, in order to pay off his creditors. As to his deficiency in the power of moral indignation, is not this found in almost all persons who write novels, or indeed who contemplate human nature from the outside? I could no more reproach such persons with taking an indulgent view of the moral infirmities of our poor human nature than I could blame a surgeon for guarding himself against feeling excessive sympathy for his patients, and for taking what is called a *professional* view of even the gravest disorders." And, in confirmation of my opinion, I called Mr. Gladstone's attention to a passage which tends to show that biographers as well as novelists are apt to take a *professional* view of moral shortcomings. The passage occurs in Plutarch's *Lives of Agis and Cleomenes*, where, after making mention of the extraordinary moral lapse which dishonoured the old age of Aratus, the biographer goes on to say: "This that we have written of Aratus (who was indued with many noble virtues, and a worthy Græcian) is not so much to accuse him, as to make us to see the frayelty and weakenes of man's nature:

the which, though it have never so excellent vertues, can not yet bring forth such perfit frute, but that it hath ever some mayme and bleamishe." (*North's Plutarch.*)

Going back to Homer, Mr. Gladstone contended that in the Iliad the Greeks were never charged with doing anything very wrong.

T.—"What do you say of the vindictiveness of Achilles?"

Mr. Gladstone went through the story of Achilles from the beginning, and thought that Hector might have procured the restoration of Helen.

G.—"The Greeks were finer characters than even some of the Hebrew patriarchs. They would never have consented to such an act as the selling of Joseph to the Egyptians. Homer marks his strong disapproval of the abduction of Helen by using the word ἥρπασαν."

T.—"You will remember that Herodotus uses the same word, and yet he thought that the Greeks were altogether in the wrong."

Mr. Gladstone seemed surprised, so I quoted in the original the passage, which says of such women as Helen: "It is plain that, if they had not wished it, they would not have been carried off," remarking that this sentence seemed to me very quaint.

G.—"Yes, of course, she consented to some extent, as is shown by the deep contrition which she expresses in the Odyssey. But was she worse than Bathsheba?"

Referring to Butler's *Analogy*, he said that he

thought Dr. James Martineau had, in some respect, unconsciously misrepresented Butler. I replied that Jowett is reported to have described Butler's work as a "tissue of false analogies"; and I quoted what he had said to me, namely, that he recoiled from the notion of attributing to a deliberate judicial act of the Deity moral anomalies similar to those which may be inseparable from the scheme of nature. Mr. Gladstone could not at all see the point of Jowett's objection. He said that there was one "audacious" passage in which Butler seemed to hint that this world may have been made as nearly perfect as the necessity of things permitted.

Something was said of the contemptuous way in which most Catholics seemed to regard Anglo-Catholics. Mr. Gladstone mentioned a Catholic Peer who compared Ritualism to mock-turtle, and who added that he preferred the real turtle. I rejoined that the antipathy felt by Romanists for what they regard as the sham Rome on the banks of the Isis reminded me of the pathetic melancholy with which Claudian contemplated the new Rome on the shores of the Bosphorus—

> "Cum subiit par Roma mihi, divisaque sumpsit
> Æquales Aurora togas."

Mr. Gladstone seemed to like this comparison.

Reverting to the *Life of Manning*, Mr. Gladstone expressed surprise that the Cardinal had said that at Harrow he had learnt many things imperfectly; and Mr. Gladstone added the amazing statement that, when he was at Eton, it was possible either to learn or not to learn, but that, if you learnt at all, you had to learn thoroughly. He wished that a good life of Busby could be written. It was of Busby that the story was told that he begged to be excused from uncovering before Charles II., because if the boys once saw him owning his inferiority to mortal man, they would lose all respect for him.

G.—"He seems to have been the parent of our public schools system; and, if that system were removed, it would be like knocking a front tooth out of our English social life. I am glad to have been at Eton, and especially to have been there under Keate. Keate was a very short man, and was conscious of thus being at a disadvantage in inspiring the boys with awe. He resorted to two expedients for counteracting this defect. First, he wore a cassock and flowing robes; and, secondly, he gave the boys the impression of always being in a passion."

With Mr. Gladstone's description of Keate it may be worth while to compare that given by Kinglake:—

" Anybody without the least notion of drawing could still draw a speaking, nay scolding, likeness of Keate. If you had no pencil, you could draw him well enough with the poker, or the leg of a chair, or the smoke of a candle. He was little more (if more at all) than five feet in height, and was not very great in girth, but within this space was concentrated the pluck of ten battalions. He had a really noble voice, and this he could modulate with great skill; but he had also the power of quacking like an angry duck, and he almost always adopted this mode of communication in order to inspire respect. He was a capital scholar, but his ingenuous learning had *not* 'softened his manners,' and *had* 'permitted them to be fierce'—tremendously fierce. He had such a complete command over his temper—I mean, over his *good* temper, that he scarcely ever allowed it to appear: you could not put him out of humour—that is, out of the *ill*-humour which he thought to be fitting for a head-master. His red shaggy eyebrows were so prominent, that he habitually used them as arms and hands for the purpose of pointing out any object towards which he wished to direct attention ; the rest of his features were equally striking in their way, and were all and all his own. He wore a fancy dress, partly resembling the costume of Napoleon, and partly that of a widow woman. I could not have named anybody more decidedly differing in appearance from the rest of the human race."

I quoted Vaughan's saying (reported to me on direct authority), viz. that it was a great advantage to him as a schoolmaster that, when he was most angry with a boy, he seemed most calm and self-possessed.

G.—"There was one excellent institution at Eton in my time. About once a week Keate summoned the boys and gave them a lecture about things in general. Whenever they were displeased they called out 'OO, OO, OO,' without moving their lips, so that Keate could not tell which boys were making the noise. There was something Homeric in this. When the Trojans murmured, it is said that they κελάδησαν, whereas Homer applies a more respectful word to the applause of the Achæans."

He did not say whether the choice of these words, as of some of the Homeric epithets, may not have been due to the exigencies of metre.

G.—"I am sorry to learn that this good old Eton custom has died out."

10

T.—" Vaughan would certainly not have tolerated it at Harrow."

G.—" What could he have done ? If he had left off giving the lectures, it would have been a triumph for the boys."

T.—" He sometimes deprived the whole school of a half-holiday for less offences than that. By the way, the compliment you paid to Busby startled me. Do you not consider Arnold the great reformer of modern public schools ? "

G.—" I doubt whether much of his influence reached Eton. I consider the three men who have recently done most for the religious improvement of Eton to have been Hawtrey, Selwyn (afterwards the well-known bishop), and the Duke of Newcastle, who founded the Newcastle Scholarship."

T.—" How has the Newcastle Scholarship promoted the religious improvement of Eton ? "

G.—" There are some divinity questions ; and the competition stimulates the candidates to learn the rudiments of theology in a way in which they would not learn them otherwise."

Jan. 18*th.*—Mr. Gladstone came to tea.

G.—" In my younger days I was a great deal in Scotland, and looked upon Presbyterianism as of all religions the least susceptible of change. But all is now different. The Free Church has taken up the traditions of Presbyterianism, and indirectly, if it has not devitalised the Established Kirk, has at least deprived it of some of its essential characteristics. The Established Kirk is in some particulars approaching the Church of England. I believe that its congregations sometimes sing Newman's hymn, " Lead, kindly Light," which would have been Anathema in my youth; and there is even some talk of their having bishops."

In illustration of the state of opinion that prevailed in Scotland during his youth or middle life, he mentioned that in a Scotch town (I think Perth) he once saw a procession of choristers, and had the curiosity to ask another Scotch boy what those boys were. " They are Puseyites." " And what are Puseyites?" " Next door to Papists." I told the story that in my younger days a captain of militia, when enlisting a recruit, asked what was his religion. " Are you a Protestant?" " Noa." " Then are you a Catholic?" " Noa." " Then what the devil are you? — Are you a heathen?" " Noa, I'm a Puseyite." The captain, after ascertaining what this latter term meant, decided that he should be sent to the Catholic service in the morning, and to the Protestant in the afternoon.

G. (laughing)—" Was that in England?"

T.—" Yes; in Chester. The story was told me at the time by one of the captains."

Mr. Gladstone spoke a good deal about Manning, whom he regarded with very mixed feelings. He still had the remains of an ardent personal affection for the Cardinal, and an admiration for his statesmanlike abilities. But the feelings were tempered by a dislike of his policy, and (as he expressed it) of his " craft." He had the strongest aversion to the Ultramontane movement. I said that a Catholic priest of liberal tendencies rejoiced at the decree of the Vatican Council in 1870, on the ground seemingly that the Pope—that is, the Church—is now released from the trammels of the past, and can embark on a career of progress.

G.—"That means that he prefers personal to constitutional authority. Would he have liked the government of the Tudors better than the government of the Plantagenets?"

Personally, I should have thought that, if compelled to choose between living under the Plantagenets on the one hand, and, on the other hand, living either at the beginning of the reign of Henry VII. or at the end of the reign of Elizabeth,—that is, during those portions of the Tudor *régime* which were comparatively exempt from religious troubles, —most of us would have given a decided preference to the England of the Tudors.

At the risk of appearing at once cynical and captious, I will offer another comment on the opinion expressed by Mr. Gladstone. In our view of nations, as of individuals of all sorts, it is not always by their periods of perfect sanity and soundness that we are most attracted. Assuredly the aloe is not in a healthy state when it flowers, any more than is the legendary swan when it sings. But I had rather contemplate either of those living things in its brief moribund glory, than during its protracted spell of salubrious dulness. And, for a like reason, I feel a greater interest in the Roman Republic as it was in the age of Cicero and of Lucretius, than as it was in the robuster epoch of Scipio and of Fabius; thus, too, *mutatis mutandis*, even were I to grant all that Mr. Gladstone claimed for the orderly sway of the Plantagenets, I should still be more drawn towards the England of Shakespeare, and of Raleigh, even than towards the England of Chaucer.

I mentioned a fact related by the aforesaid priest, and quoted in my *Memoir of Jowett*. It is there stated (p. 27) that the priest wrote to me :—

"Did I ever tell you of a saying of Cardinal Manning on the hell question ? A friend suggesting that it was a place of eternal suffering eternally untenanted, he answered: 'If one did not hope that it was so, who could endure life ?'" According to this ingenious theory, impenitent sinners are indirectly suggestive of Dryden's hind; for they are *doomed to hell, but fated not to burn.* But Mr. Gladstone did not see his way either to granting them an escape from the nether fires, or to investing them with the insensibility of the salamander. And indeed, when the Cardinal's merciful special pleading was reported to him, he emphatically replied that the report seemed to him hard to believe. He went on to speak of an article which he had written about Butler's chapter on a future life. He had no sympathy with the belief in natural immortality. That belief, he contended, was upheld only by Plato and a few other philosophers in pagan times. It is nowhere to be found in the Bible; and Origen was, he believed, the earliest Christian writer who adopted it; afterwards it became so widespread, if not universal, that Servetus, when accused, amongst other things, of the heresy of attacking that belief, openly declared: "If ever I said that, and not only said it, but published it, and infected the whole world, I would condemn myself to death."

G.—"Do you believe in natural immortality?"

T.—"I certainly wish to believe it. I am naturally disposed in favour of any form of the belief in immortality which does not involve the belief in final retribution."

G.—"But the belief in natural immortality is not inconsistent with the belief in final retribution."

In strict theory, I suppose that he was right. But, practically, the scientific objections to the belief in natural immortality are so formidable that this belief is obliged in self-defence to throw itself, as it were, on our highest aspirations; and those aspirations undoubtedly point to the elevating hope that good will be the final goal of ill. Probably Lord Sherbrooke had some such thought in his mind when he said, in conversation, "I utterly refuse to believe in a God who is worse than I am." Whereto he might have added as a corollary: "I utterly refuse to believe in a future life which is worse than the present life." Yes; this is the universal postulate of enlightened theology: *De Diis nil nisi bonum.*

Wishing to see what Mr. Gladstone would make of the obvious objections to the belief in personal immortality, I expounded them as clearly as I could; and, with that view, I gave him the substance of a conversation which had taken place between Professor Tyndall and myself, and which has so much intrinsic interest that I will venture to repeat it here:—

In 1886 (or thereabouts) I remarked to Professor Tyndall that Dr. Maudsley somewhere speaks of Mind as "a function of brain, or rather of organisation." " Do you suppose," Tyndall asked, laughing, "that Maudsley is the only man who says that?" He clearly regarded the point as one on which rational biologists are agreed. I then inquired whether he did not find it hard to reconcile this opinion with the belief in immortality. " If the brain is the organ, and consciousness is merely the function, is it not contrary to all analogy to expect that, in this instance, the function will outlast the organ? Is it not like imagining that the fire will go on burning when the fuel is exhausted? Huxley would doubtless agree with you on the general principle ; and therefore I am puzzled to find him taking a purely Agnostic attitude on the question. He says, in effect, that, if people tell him that they believe in immortality, he asks them on what they ground their belief; and, if they tell him that they disbelieve in it, he asks them on what they ground their disbelief." In reply, Tyndall took exception to my illustration drawn from fire and fuel. He said that there is no evidence that consciousness, like heat or electricity, is a mode of motion ; but he spoke of consciousness as " dependent " on organisation.

Tol.—" Does not the word ' dependent ' involve the whole issue ? "

Tyn. (after a pause)—" Do you suppose that, if Huxley had been in this room now, and you had pressed him as you have pressed me, he would seriously maintain that the balance lies evenly between the two opposite hypotheses ? "

He went on to make it quite clear that, in his opinion, the view of Lucretius that

> " animi natura nequit sine corpore oriri
> Sola, neque a nervis et sanguine longiter esse,"

is in all probability correct. Presently Tyndall added, with a smile, "Huxley does sometimes throw sops to Cerberus"—meaning, doubtless, that this *economy of truth,* or *economy of logic,* was practised unconsciously. That such a comment should have been made by Tyndall, even playfully, on his admired and admirable friend, will surprise some readers more, perhaps, than it surprised me. In explanation of what he said, I will add that, long before this conversation had taken place, and indeed shortly after Huxley had published his essay on "Administrative Nihilism," I called Tyndall's attention to one or two of Huxley's unexpected utterances, utterances which, though certainly not orthodox, had something dogmatically and aggressively anti-materialistic in their tone. "His mind," replied Tyndall, " is a pendulum which has been going into one extreme, and now inclines towards the opposite one."

After hearing what I had to say, Mr. Gladstone expressed strong disagreement with Tyndall. " Scientific men," he exclaimed, "talk a great deal too confidently about many points ; and this is one of them." When I insisted that, according to Tyndall, mind is a function of the brain, just as sight is the function of the eye, he interrupted me: " I beg your pardon, sight is *not* the function of the eye."

T.—" At anyrate, you will admit that the eye is the organ of sight."

G.—" Strictly speaking, the eye is the carrier of sight." I confess that this objection of his seemed to me very hypercritical, all the more so because, so far as it goes, it rather strengthens than weakens the case for what is called Materialism. Let us grant that the brain is the organ of sight, and that the eye is the mere servant of the brain. The decomposition of the eye extinguishes sight. What vital function, then, will be left when the brain is decomposed ?   To speak broadly : If the death of the servant puts a stop to his peculiar form of service, what form of service would be possible when the master and all the servants have perished together ? I was casting about for some safer topic when, suddenly remembering what had recently passed between us about wit and humour, I stumbled on the highly original observation that Charles Lamb seemed to me humorous rather than witty ! But Mr. Gladstone, of course, held the rudder ; and, after drily assenting to what may be termed my leading platitude, he turned our course away from the smooth water and steered straight towards the Day of Judgment. He began by saying that the Christian doctrine of immortality was that of union with God ; and, by way of illustration, he quoted the text, " As Thou, Father, art in Me, and I in Thee, that they also may be one in us."   He then repeated his conviction that natural immortality is not to be found in the New Testament.   I pointed out, on the lines laid down by Renan, the difference between the Platonic view of Immortality and the Christian view of the Resurrection of the Body.   I repeated what Renan says to the effect that there are at least two distinct views of Immortality.   There is the Greek view, which divides man into two parts, body and soul, and which represents the soul as surviving without the body ; this view seems to be entertained by the author of Ecclesiastes, who says, "Then shall the dust return to the earth as it was : and the spirit shall return unto God, who gave it." On the other hand, there is the distinctively Christian view of the Resurrection of the Body, which does not assign to the soul an independent existence, but pronounces that soul and body together shall be raised at the last day. Mr. Gladstone seemed to agree; but, on my saying that one or two texts are not so easily reconciled with this opinion, he asked, " Which texts ?" I quoted the words addressed to the dying thief; and added that this text certainly implied that the thief's soul would be in heaven while his body was decomposing in the earth.

G.—" Oh, there is no doubt that the New Testament teaches throughout that the souls of the righteous will go to heaven immediately after their death."

T.—" If the righteous are to be severed from the wicked immediately after death, what need will there be for a Day of Judgment ? Would it not be a strange anomaly that the dying thief and Dives should be called upon at the last day to make their defence before the Tribunal of God, if each of them, the former in Paradise and the latter in ' torments,' has already learnt by experience what the final sentence on him is to be ? Would not the condemned be entitled (adapting a famous line) to say of such a proceeding : ' 'Tis like a *trial* after execution ' ?"

I fear that I cannot have made my reasoning plain to Mr. Gladstone; for he answered with unusual heat, "I really cannot answer such questions. The Almighty never took me into His confidence as to why there is to be a Day of Judgment." I felt it was impossible to press the matter further, and merely said something to the effect that the expectation of the immediate end of the world probably deterred the apostles from laying much stress on the condition of the dead in the interval before the general Resurrection.

Sir John Seeley somewhere, while expressing his strong wish to retain the belief in immortality, has spoken of the belief in the Day of Judgment as indicating a certain want of culture in those who maintain it. He was of course referring to his own contemporaries; and his remark would not have applied to persons who, like Mr Gladstone, were a quarter of a century older. In Mr. Gladstone's mind this unsightly and withered branch of the popular theology was as fixed as in the minds of the congregation whom, in the days of my youth, a zealous clergyman edified by exclaiming: "In what form the Angel will appear I know no more than of what metal his trumpet will be made!" Shall I be thought disrespectful if I remark that this and one or two other sayings of Mr. Gladstone remind me of Walter Bagehot's epigrammatic assertion that, "A Constitutional Statesman is in general a man of common opinions and uncommon abilities—of the powers of a first-rate man and the creed of a second-rate man"?

Mr. Gladstone rose to depart. I was always

anxious in my conversations with him to refresh myself with a sort of old-world bath by hearing his recollections of his youth and middle life; and I was disappointed that in this instance the conversation had drifted from the past and present to the future. As I walked with him to his hotel, I observed that, as Miss Gladstone had been so long at Newnham, he had probably often considered the question of the higher education of women and of their future demands. He replied that he had considered the question very often; he was disposed to open the professions to them, but to exclude them from the franchise; if they were once given the franchise, it would be hard to prevent their having everything else.

T.—"What do you mean by 'everything else'? Do you mean that they would want to become Members of Parliament?"

G.—"Yes, and to become judges and generals."

T.—"But surely, if they want to become generals, they would be told that they were, owing to physical causes, unfit for the army."

G.—"Oh, but they would answer that, if they were physically unfit to become generals, they never would or could become generals."

T.—"Yes; this is the kind of argument which Mill illustrated by saying that no law was ever passed forbidding men with weak arms to become blacksmiths."

G.—"One concession, however, I would make to them. It seems to me perfectly scandalous that,

out of the vast incomes of our two Universities, not
a sixpence has ever been given to a woman."

T.—" Would you have women made professors ? "

G.—" There might be difficulties about that. But
they might be helpful in other ways. As compared
with men, they are handicapped in the race of life;
and they certainly ought to have their share of the
University revenues. I remember urging this on
Lightfoot at the time of the University Commission;
but he thought that it would be too fundamental a
change."

January 8th, 1896.—Dined with Mr. Armitstead
and the Gladstones; Lord and Lady Cranbourne
were present. Mr. Gladstone, speaking of the learned
divine whose reminiscences of him I have quoted
above, regretted that so excellent a man was obliged
by weak health to live abroad.

G.—" He would probably have risen to the highest
distinction in the Church."

T.—" Surely very many able clergymen, for various
reasons, do not gain ecclesiastical preferments."

G.—" No doubt that used to be the case. At the
time of the Newmanite movement, every clergyman
who took part in that movement was rigorously
placed under a ban. But things are changed
now."

I spoke of Jowett as a very distinguished clergyman, who never received ecclesiastical preferment;
and the conversation drifted to Jowett's Sermon on
Discourse. I said that on that occasion he chose a

very odd text. A sermon is generally supposed to bear some relation to the text in its original sense; and in this instance the selection of " *Man shall not live by bread alone, but by every word that proceedeth out of the mouth,*"[1] suggests the notion that the dialogue with the Arch-fiend in the wilderness had turned on the best mode of being agreeable in society. Mr. Gladstone smiled, and acknowledged that sometimes Jowett's texts were certainly peculiar; but, on the whole, the sermons seemed to him to be very interesting and striking. He then came up to me with his edition of Butler's *Analogy*, and said, "This is my Butler." As I have to wear very peculiar spectacles, the field of my vision is limited; and Mr. Gladstone happened to hold the book outside that field. I therefore did not see the book; but, chancing to see a gentleman in evening dress advancing towards me, I imagined that this must be the butler, who was in all probability bringing me my handkerchief, which I might have dropped on the staircase. This trivial incident is worth recording, as the mistake would scarcely have been made but for that peculiar inelastic and, so to say, stereotyped earnestness of manner which made it hard sometimes to tell whether Mr. Gladstone was speaking on a grave or on a light topic.

At dinner the conversation began with the rainfall at Biarritz; and I took the opportunity of raising the question whether a dry or a damp climate is the more favourable to longevity.

[1] The text is thus truncated by Jowett.

G.—"There are some very curious facts about longevity. I will mention one. The proportion of centenarians in Scotland is about double of what it is in England, and in Ireland it is about double of what it is in Scotland."

I asked whether that might not be due to the exaggeration of very old people. Were the registers as carefully kept in Ireland and Scotland as in England?

G.—"I am speaking of the most recent returns."

I asked whether the registers were kept with equal care in all three countries a hundred years ago, and reminded Mr. Gladstone of the difficulty which arises when one child dies and another, born some years later, is called by the same name.

G.—"I know that; but I think that this cause of error would exist equally in the three countries. The result seems to me very remarkable indeed." He went on to talk about Sir G. Cornwall Lewis, for whose judgment, except on matters of "finance," he had the highest respect; but in his scepticism about centenarianism he was, in Mr. Gladstone's opinion, simply wrong. I adverted to my conversation with Sir G. Cornwall Lewis (reported in *Safe Studies*, pp. 37–43), which occurred only a few weeks before his death, and in which he admitted that a few cases of centenarianism were established.

G.—"It appears, then, that, like the vaccinators, he changed his ground."

T.—"How have vaccinators changed their ground?"

G.—"They began by saying that, if you are once

vaccinated, you will never have small-pox; then they said that you must be vaccinated twice; and then that you must be vaccinated once in seven years!"

T.—"But I suppose that nearly all doctors are in favour of vaccination."

G.—"Yes; ninety-nine out of every hundred. But at one time medical opinion was in favour of inoculation. Indeed, they were very nearly making inoculation compulsory; whereas now it is penal."[1]

T.—"But does not vaccination greatly diminish small-pox?"

G.—"Yes; but it has greatly increased the tendency to zymotic diseases. Whenever there is a zymotic tendency in the child from which the lymph is taken, that disease is transmitted to the vaccinated child. I should have been afraid to tell my old friend, Sir Andrew Clark, that I always feel a strong repulsion to seeing the clear, pure skin of a child made to break out into pustules."

T.—"But are you opposed to vaccination?"

G.—"No; but I dislike the idea of its being compulsory. I don't like the notion of the State stepping in between parent and child when it is not absolutely necessary. The State is generally a very bad nurse."

---

[1] There is a passage in *She Stoops to Conquer* which, even when allowance is made for comic exaggeration, shows how prevalent, in Goldsmith's day, was the belief in the beneficial effects of inoculation. "I vow," says Mrs. Hardcastle, "since inoculation began, there is no such thing to be seen as a plain woman." *O fortunatæ nimium !*

T.—" If vaccinators have made a change of front, so, too, have thought-readers and *clairvoyants.*   At one time it was said that, if you could hypnotise me, I might be able to inform you on topics previously unknown either to you or to me.   It is now, I understand, merely said that what is in your mind may through some mysterious process be passed on to mine."

G.—" I keep my judgment in suspense about thought-reading.   I don't let myself be entangled in the belief in it; but I am not violently opposed to it.   There seems to be very strong evidence for the stories of second sight at the moment of death."

He then gave an account of an old and faithful servant of his own, who took to drinking, suddenly decamped, and afterwards destroyed himself.   On the morning after his disappearance Mr. Gladstone thought that he saw him waiting at the breakfast-table, and asked the butler whether he was not there. Mr. Gladstone had no reason to think that this occurred at the moment of the servant's death; but he said it was the only occasion on which he re-membered himself to have been the victim of an ocular delusion.   One or two instances bearing on the question of second sight were told by a lady at table; and she was advised by him to submit the facts to the Psychical Society.   I told the story of a lady whose son died in Australia.   She gave me the following account of what occurred: Though she knew that he was at the Antipodes, she suddenly heard his voice calling " Mother," and mentioned the fact to her daughter. They took a note of the time, which was 5 p.m., and they afterwards learnt that "at that very moment he died." I presently led her on to say that it was at 5 p.m. that he had died. So she evidently had not made allowance for the difference between English and Australian time. On my subsequently cross-questioning the daughter, I learnt that the mother's attention had been called to this difference, but that she persisted in telling the story in the old way. Also, to the best of the daughter's recollection, it was a mere hallucination of her mother's that she had mentioned the fact at the time to her. If, under the influence of strong emotion, the wish to believe could produce actual belief in this somewhat extreme instance, might not the same cause be expected to produce belief in other instances? The sorrowing friends who tell such tales are in a mythopœic, and, as Burns would have said, "ghaist-alluring" frame of mind; and for obvious reasons it is generally hard, if not impossible, to cross-question them. Mr. Gladstone listened; but evidently thought that my explanation would not cover all the cases.

T.—"Suppose that the watchword, after being given to a sentinel, was discovered by the enemy, and that there was no possible way of accounting for the discovery except on the hypothesis either of treachery or of thought-reading."

G. (*smiling*)—"If I was the General, I should have the sentinel shot.' But he said nothing about the significance of such a case as a sort of negative evidence against thought-reading.

He reverted to what was then his engrossing topic, *Manning's Life*.

G.—" The worst of nearly all biographies is that they contain hardly anything but praise."

T.—" Is not that inevitable ? The facts must be furnished by the family of the deceased, and the biographer feels bound to consider their feelings."

G.—" This may explain the unfortunate rule, but only adds value to such an exception as Purcell's Life of the Cardinal. Another great exception is Froude's Life of Carlyle."

T.—" Some would say that Froude went into the opposite extreme. Do you not think Trevelyan's *Life of Macaulay* is an excellent piece of work ? "

G.—" Yes ; but he had no great difficulties to contend with. By the way, I once asked Döllinger, whose literary discernment impressed me more than that of any other man, what he thought of Macaulay's very peculiar style. I wanted to know how that style would strike a foreigner. Döllinger did not seem to see the exact point of my question, but answered : ' I should admire Macaulay more if I was quite sure that he was not misleading me.' " I quoted Charles Austin's *candid-friendly* remark to Macaulay : " You always have by you some white and some black paint ; when you describe a Tory, you put on the black paint ; and, when you describe a Whig, the white."

G.—"I am sure that Macaulay was not consciously unfair; but he was not impartial, like Hallam."

T.—"You will remember what Macaulay said about Sir James Macintosh and Hallam. He thought that they were both eminently impartial; but that Macintosh was always inclined to indulgence, whilst Hallam was a hanging judge."

G.—"Perhaps Hallam's judgments are a little severe; but, on the whole, they are wonderfully just."

T.—"Did you ever read the very touching words which he wrote on the tomb of his son Arthur?"

G.—"Did he not use an Italian phrase?"

T.—"I was thinking of the Latin epitaph." And I proceeded, as nearly as I could remember, to quote the words:

"Vale, dulcissime
Vale, dilectissime desideratissime,
Requiescas in pace,
Pater ac Mater hic posthac requiescamus tecum
Usque ad tubam."

T.—"Charles Austin was surprised at Hallam's use of such very orthodox phraseology as that contained in the last three words."

G.—"Charles Austin may have been surprised, but I am not. Hallam was a thorough Christian."

T.—"You knew Arthur Hallam; did you not?"

G.—"Very well indeed. He was my greatest friend at Eton. Though we lived at some distance from each other, we used to breakfast each with the other on alternate weeks. He was quite the most rising man that I knew. He was so much above and beyond all the rest of us "—here he lifted up his arm with a symbolical gesture—"that I wondered how he could manage to deal with us."

I asked what was Arthur Hallam's age at the time of his death; and Mr. Gladstone showed how fresh everything about him was in his own memory by stating the month when he was born and the month when he died.

T.—"I suppose that you are a great admirer of *In Memoriam.*"

G.—"Yes. It is obscure in parts; but, on the whole, I admire it very much."

Something was said about Tennyson's extreme sensitiveness. Mr. Gladstone admitted that he was sensitive; but he added that, for all that, Tennyson did not mind telling a story against himself. The poet himself had mentioned that long ago a friend of his, going to Freshwater, asked a rustic to tell him who were the chief inhabitants. On the names being mentioned of several persons not known to fame, the stranger inquired about Mr. Tennyson. "We don't think much of him," was the reply; "he keeps only one man-servant, and *he* sleeps out!" I capped this anecdote by mentioning that Tennyson had rather enjoyed telling the following story against Carlyle. Carlyle had gone to Cambridge during the long vacation, and, finding a stray undergraduate, asked him the names of some of the Colleges. The young man kindly acted as *cicerone*, and did the honours of Cambridge. On parting,

Carlyle said to him, "Thank you, young man. Perhaps you may like to know that you have rendered a service to Thomas Carlyle!" Looking somewhat surprised, this Verdant Green, jun., answered affably, "Indeed, Mr. Thomas Carlyle, I am very glad to show Cambridge to a gentleman who has never seen it before." One would like to have seen, or (better still) to have *thought-read*, Carlyle when the simple-minded undergraduate said that. Mr. Gladstone remarked that he thought that "Guinevere" was the one of Tennyson's poems that he liked best, and asked which was my favourite. After mentioning "St. Agnes' Eve," "Œnone," and the "Passing of Arthur" as the shorter poems which particularly attract me, I said that it seems to me very interesting to contrast the tone of the earlier and of the later "Locksley Hall."

G.—"The second 'Locksley Hall' appears to me to make too gloomy a forecast. I wrote a criticism of it in the *Nineteenth Century.*"

T.—"Are you not inclined to take a thoroughly sanguine view of the prospects of this very reforming age?"

G.—"Not altogether. The future is to me a blank. I cannot at all guess what is coming."

T.—"Do you mean that you are afraid that Democracy may bring everything to a dead level, or that Science is too hastily moving the old theological landmarks?"

G.—"I am not so much afraid either of Democracy or of Science as of the love of money. This seems

to me to be a growing evil.   Also, there is a danger
from the growth of that dreadful military spirit."

I asked him if he thought that, as is often said,
the perfecting of the art of war will make wars more
terrible, and therefore more dreaded; so that *Suis
et ipsa bella viribus ruent.*   He seemed uncertain.

T.—"Is not the moral standard of public men
higher than it used to be?"

G.—"I should say that in England the change
has been all the other way.   About the Continent
I am not so sure. *(After a pause.)*   Since the retirement of Bismarck, Crispi would probably rank as
the first of continental statesmen.   I am no great
admirer of the public career either of Castlereagh
or of Metternich.   But, judging as a moralist, I
should say that the careers of Castlereagh and of
Metternich would compare favourably with those of
Bismarck and Crispi."   Being asked by another of
the party what he thought of Bismarck, he replied,
" He is a very big man, but very unscrupulous."

When Mr. Gladstone thus acknowledged that
statesmanship had declined, the admission seemed to
me suggestive and significant.   Was there not also a
gradual decline of political ability during the great
century of Athens?   Were not the politicians of the
time of Cleon smaller men than those either of the
time of Themistocles or of the time of Pericles?
And may not the deterioration of Athenian statesmanship in the fourth century B.C., and that of
European statesmanship in the nineteenth century
A.D., be due in part to the same cause, namely, the

advance of Democracy? Or, to speak more precisely, do we not commonly find a goodlier fellowship of heroes and patriots when aristocracy and democracy are militant than when either aristocracy or democracy is triumphant? And, after all, are we not thus brought face to face with one of the aspects of the too familiar question whether, just as each one of us must expect his own physical strength, sooner or later, to dwindle and decay, even so the time must come to every civilised nation when the advancing tide of scepticism will bring destruction on public confidence, and indeed on belief in ideals of all sorts?

$$\phi\theta\acute{\iota}\nu\epsilon\iota\ \mu\grave{\epsilon}\nu\ \acute{\iota}\sigma\chi\grave{\upsilon}s\ \gamma\hat{\eta}s,\ \phi\theta\acute{\iota}\nu\epsilon\iota\ \delta\grave{\epsilon}\ \sigma\acute{\omega}\mu\alpha\tau os,$$
$$\theta\nu\acute{\eta}\sigma\kappa\epsilon\iota\ \delta\grave{\epsilon}\ \pi\acute{\iota}\sigma\tau\iota s,\ \beta\lambda\alpha\sigma\tau\acute{\alpha}\nu\epsilon\iota\ \delta'\ \grave{\alpha}\pi\iota\sigma\tau\acute{\iota}\alpha.$$

But, though such reflections obtruded themselves upon me, I feared to embark on deep and stormy controversies,—*ne parva Tyrrhenum per æquor vela darem,*—and I kept my musings to myself. Presently Mr. Gladstone concluded with the melancholy observation: " Nowhere does the ideal enter so little as into politics; nowhere does human conduct fall so far below the highest ethical standard. I did not always think this; but I am convinced of it now." It is noteworthy that Mr. Gladstone's great rival has given utterance to an opinion which, though differently expressed, is seemingly of like import. "There is nothing," says Disraeli, "in which the power of circumstance is more evident than in politics." After the ladies left the room, the conversation turned on the Premiership of Disraeli and on the ethical questions involved in Lord Salisbury's acceptance of office under him, and in the late Lord Derby's resignation. From this part of our discourse I will only select one remark. "I am convinced," said Mr. Gladstone, "that acceptance of office is apt to be less sharply criticised than resignation. The motives which induce a man to resign are more severely scrutinised than those which induce a man to accept." The conversation passed on to the art of oratory. One of the party mentioned that Sheridan is said to have put off preparing the Begum Speech to the last, and then to have devoted three nights to it. Surely this was not the way to be in trim for a great speech.

G.—"No. Of course it was a fault; but the fault was on the right side. I have never found it succeed to prepare a speech long before. A speech so prepared is sure to lack freshness; and freshness is a great element of success."

Mr. Gladstone did not want the number of lawyers in the House of Commons to be increased: "They are too fond of putting their hands into the public purse. The chief exception to this rule was Jessel the Jew!"

February 8th.—Mr. Gladstone liked the review of his *Butler* in the *Athenæum*. His critic sought to discredit the chronology of the Bible. He himself tried to defend it by speaking of that of the Septuagint as probably based on more trustworthy MSS. than those from which the Hebrew text is derived. He made the odd remark that, not merely the Hebrews, but the Chinese and Hindoos, did not claim millions of years for the antiquity of man. He tried to distinguish biblical man from geological man. It seemed to him not merely an "error," but "nonsense," on the part of men of science to affirm that the Greeks had descended from any race as low as the Esquimaux. I replied that, holding this opinion, he must presumably think it still greater nonsense for men of science to affirm that the old Greeks could have been descended from such a creature as the ourang-outang. He answered vaguely that he was not prepared to deny that the Greeks might have ultimately come from protoplasm. What he complained of was that men of science were so confident in their assertions about the Ascent of Man. He passed on from this to the development of the colour sense. He reminded me that he had often contended that this sense was very imperfect in Homer. Homer had such an exquisite sense of the beauty of form, but seems strangely confused when speaking of colour. An eminent Jewish Rabbi had told him that the colour sense was also deficient amongst the old Hebrews. In the text in Psalm lxviii. 13, " Yet shall ye be as the wings of a dove covered with silver, and her feathers like yellow gold," the concluding words should be "*green* leaflets of gold."

T.—" Macaulay, in the introduction to one of his *Lays*, remarks that in our early national songs all the gold is red. The primitive colour blindness, if such it was, seems to have taken a variety of forms."

G.—"Undoubtedly. And yet my opinions on this subject drew on me the anathemas of Darwinian orthodoxy. Did you know there was such a thing as Darwinian orthodoxy ?"

T.—"I am not sure. But, by way of parallel, I may mention that, many years ago, a near kinswoman of Cobden complained to me of Mill's unorthodoxy; and that, on my saying to her something vague about the unorthodox views of many modern philosophers, she startled me by the interruption, 'Oh, I am not referring to unorthodoxy of that sort. I mean that he is *unorthodox in Political Economy.*'"

G. (smiling)—"That may illustrate what I mean. Some German Evolutionists said that I *must* be wrong, because some of the lower animals can be shown to have a well-developed sense of colour; and what they have, man must have."

T.—"Those Evolutionists talk great nonsense. They might as well say that, as birds and butterflies have wings, man must have them too. The answer would, of course, be that the organs in question had been atrophied by disuse. I am reminded of Pope's couplet—

> 'Why has not man a microscopic eye ?
> For this plain reason—man is not a fly.'

Goethe had said—no doubt, speaking metaphorically —that the prolonged use of either the telescope or the microscope interferes with the normal use of the eye. And so likewise, if man had microscopic vision or any faculty utterly alien to his ordinary requirements, those ordinary requirements would tend to be neglected."

G.—"The controversy about the colour sense is still going on in Germany; but in fairness I must say that the majority of German writers do not seem to agree with me. I may mention one fact. I went into a children's hospital, and, observing that they were dressed in bright colours, I asked why this was, and was told that they preferred bright colours. I then asked at what age they began to show the preference, and was told that they showed it before they were a twelvemonth old."

The conversation turned on the Jews, on their comparative immunity from certain diseases, and on the contradictory accounts of the comparative longevity of Jews and Gentiles. Mr. Gladstone thought highly of the Jews, and said that Sir Andrew Clark, who had many Jewish patients, thought well of them morally. Mr. Gladstone had at one time gone into the question of the feeling entertained against pork by many Orientals. He consulted the two most learned men of his acquaintance, Döllinger and Lord Acton; but these could tell him nothing about it. At last he thought he had obtained a clue. Whenever Homer speaks about the eating of pigs, it is always in connection with some Orientals. Pigs were eaten wholesale by the suitors of Penelope; but Mr. Gladstone considered that the Ithacans were of Oriental or, as Homer would have said, of

Phœnician descent. Indeed, he thought it significant that Homer had made his two Protagonists, Achilles and Odysseus, the former of Hellenic, the latter of Phœnician descent. Two things struck Mr. Gladstone about Orientals in reference to the pig. Their laws were constantly forbidding them to eat it; and they were constantly breaking those laws.

T.—" Why are these two conditions found more among early Orientals than among early Europeans ? "

G.—" Eating pork seems to be more liable to produce trichinosis in the East than in the West. On the other hand, Orientals found a pig diet very economical and convenient."

T.—" Why did not Europeans find it equally convenient ? "

G.—" I don't know whether at that early time the domestic pig was common in Europe, though the wild boar seems to have been known. The cat, likewise, does not seem to have made its way into Europe in the earliest times. With regard to the Jews, I am inclined to believe, with Max Müller, that their great intellectual development did not occur until after they had been brought into contact with Aryan influences, that is, not until after the writing of the Septuagint."

T.—" How, then, do you account for the genius of Isaiah ? "

G.—" You must remember that Isaiah wrote under very peculiar conditions. I could give an example, within my own experience, of the wonderful intellectual results which strong excitement may bring about. The prophets wrote under spiritual excitement of the strongest kind, which was, in fact, what we call inspiration. Many passages in their writings and many of the Psalms have the greatest possible fascination for me, but I am confident that none of these old Hebrew writers could have produced the poems of Homer or the plays of Æschylus."

Personally, I should have thought that the difference between the two forms of literary excellence was a difference rather of kind than of degree; Homer could no more have written like Isaiah than Isaiah could have written like Homer. I own I was much surprised at finding myself in this instance (so to say) more on the side of the Bible than Mr. Gladstone was. Did not his words in this instance seem to indicate a natural, as opposed to a supernatural, view of inspiration? Was it not remarkable that the Greeks, without supernatural aid, could write better than the Hebrews with supernatural aid?

I begged Mr. Gladstone to tell me the personal experience to which he had referred. He replied that he had been member for Newark at the time of the passing of the Poor Law in 1834. The new law aroused the strongest antagonism. He heard some of the people say, " I would rather clem [starve] than go to the workhouse." One day he saw in the Nottingham newspaper a tragic account of the murder of four children by their father.

The father confessed his guilt, and explained how he had strangled them all to prevent the risk of their having to end their days in the workhouse. The poor man, in describing the feelings which had led him to commit this atrocious act, was animated by such an intensity of passion, and used such burning words, that Mr. Gladstone was at the time reminded of the description of Ugolino in Dante, a passage which he regarded as the finest in the *Inferno*, if not in the entire *Divina Commedia*.

I called his attention to what seemed to me the most conspicuous of all examples of the way in which an extraordinary stimulus may be given to literature and art. The literary glory of Athens may be roughly said to have been confined to the century and a half after the battle of Marathon. It is hard to think that, during that period, the natural and hereditary qualities of the Athenians were much superior to those of other Greeks.

G.—" Can that be so? Surely an Athenian child was far better endowed by nature than a Spartan child."

T.—" If an Athenian child received from nature far higher qualities than a Spartan or, let us say, a Bœotian child, how are we to account for the fact that before the fifth century B.C. Bœotia had produced at least two poets of the first order, while Attica had apparently not produced even one?"

Mr. Gladstone admitted that he could not solve this difficulty. He merely remarked that, in his opinion, too little notice was taken of some of the earlier Greek poets; and thus he presently was led back to his favourite, Homer. He quoted the familiar Latin line about the seven cities which contended for the honour of having been Homer's birthplace: "Smyrna, Rhodos, Colophon, Salamis, Chios, Argos, Athenæ," and he also repeated Heywood's couplet—

> "Seven cities warred for Homer being dead,
> Who living had no roofe to shrowd his head."

G.—"Homer, like Shakespeare, towered so completely above all his contemporaries that there is no understanding how his age can have produced him. Do those Germans who doubt whether there was a Homer, at all remove the difficulty? Take the most moderate of the sceptics, the *chorizontes*. Does it help matters to say that one Homer may have produced the Iliad and another may have produced the Odyssey? It is hard enough to conceive how early times can have brought forth one Homer; but it would be harder still to suppose that they could have brought forth two. It is as if some critic, observing certain differences between Hamlet and Macbeth, were to declare that the Elizabethan age must have produced two Shakespeares. Really, the incredulity of sceptical critics astonishes me less than their credulity."

I had been reading Bourget's *Outre Mer* where, along with democracy and science, the sentiment of race, of nationality, is spoken of as one of the great dangers of modern civilisation. I remarked to Mr. Gladstone that this feeling of nationality is sometimes thought to have been called into activity by Louis Napoleon, who, in fact, raised the cry, " Italy for the Italians." Mr. Gladstone shook his head, and said that he was inclined to think that this sentiment was one of the legacies that we owe to the French Revolution, which certainly maintained the principle of " France for the French." He, however, acknowledged that this legacy of the Revolution was a long time in coming into active operation.

T.—" Do you not think that the great armaments on the Continent are the indirect results of the improvement in the art of war ? "

G. (smiling)—" I am amused at your patriotic reservation. Why do you say, ' on the Continent ' ? It might be contended that the sum of money spent on the army and navy in England is, as compared with the population, equal to that spent in foreign countries. In England, of course, more is expended on the navy ; and the sums spent on the building of ships must be taken into account."

I then reverted to my original point, and asked whether the improvements in the art of war do not now oblige adjacent countries to keep their forces in readiness against each other. In former times, a country whose forces were not so kept was, no doubt, at a disadvantage at the beginning of a campaign. But in those times the disadvantage was of a kind which generally admitted of being afterwards remedied. In the wars of the present day, on the other hand, the consequences of delay would probably be fatal. Mr. Gladstone agreed that there was probably a good deal in this explanation; but he added that, not being a military man, he was not prepared to say whether other causes may not have been at work. I remembered that Bourget fears that perils may be in store for America from the exotic element,—that is to say, from the great and increasing numbers of German and other immigrants who are not bound to America by any patriotic tie, and who in many instances are Socialists, if not Anarchists; did Mr. Gladstone think that there is any risk of a disruption of the Union?

G.—" I think none whatever. At the time of the American Civil War, the Union was subjected to a tremendous strain. There was a threefold antagonism; there was the opposition between the interests of some individual States and that of the Federation; between emancipation and slavery; and between Free Trade and Protection. Over these three dangers the Union triumphed; and I can see no dangers of equal magnitude to which it is now exposed."

I went on to speak of the Venezuelan dispute; and I remarked that an American politician, at once very distinguished and very friendly to England, had lately said, in a private letter, that this dispute seemed to him merely a symptom of a widespread animosity felt towards England in the States.

G.—" I very much fear that it is so. And unfortunately this is not all. We seem to be unpopular all over the world. The French dislike us. The

Dutch hate us, and naturally. The Germans showed what their feelings were by the way in which they seconded the monstrous and preposterous claim of their Emperor. Now, when an individual is disliked by all his neighbours, one naturally asks whether he has not done something to deserve his unpopularity. And, in the same way, I cannot help wondering whether, when England is so much disliked, it may not be to a great extent her own fault. Have you remarked that England has several times, of late years, submitted an international dispute to arbitration, and that the decision has generally been against her? This is to me a very unpleasant subject of reflection. The English are a very strange people. They have very great qualities; but also they have great faults."

He made a further comment on the German Emperor, which it is unnecessary to repeat. Suffice it to say that it was abundantly clear that he would fain have bestowed on his Majesty the Sophoclean benediction :—

$$\tilde{\omega} \; \pi a\hat{\imath}, \; \gamma \acute{\epsilon} \nu o\iota o \; \pi a\tau \rho \grave{o}s \; \epsilon \mathring{v}\tau v\chi \acute{\epsilon}\sigma \tau \epsilon \rho os$$
$$\tau \grave{a} \; \delta' \; \mathring{a}\lambda \lambda' \; \mathring{o}\mu o\iota os.^1$$

As he was dilating on the unpopularity of the English, a thought passed through my mind resembling one which 1 have since come across in a letter of Jowett's :—"I do not think Europe has any deep hatred of us; only a petty jealousy of our

---

1 "O child, may'st thou be more **fortunate than thy father,** but in other respects be like him !"

sleek, well-fed appearance, and satisfaction with ourselves." But, without embarking on this wide question, I asked Mr. Gladstone whether he meant that the typical Englishman is apt to flaunt the " Civis Britannicus sum " in the presence of foreigners, and to walk about the Continent (in the manner alleged against him) as if, wherever he was, the whole place belonged to him.

G.—" Yes. That is what I mean. The English are arrogant."

T.—" But is not the narrow insularity of John Bull gradually broadening as he sees more of his neighbours ? "

G.—" I trust that it is; but your political friends are doing all that they can to arrest the improvement."

T.—" Who are my political friends? Living abroad as I do, I try to keep outside politics, though no doubt I am biassed by my Conservative education and traditions."

G. (smiling)—" I remember your once calling yourself a Whig; and I know by experience that nowadays men who call themselves Whigs are nearly always supporters of the Salisbury Government ! Goodbye. God bless you."

Yes; I feel, and shall always feel, the effects of my Conservative education. And yet, now that I was bidding farewell to the great Reformer, and could not shake off the foreboding that he and I might never meet again, I asked myself whether impartial history may not judge him worthy of as splendid a eulogy as that which Ovid bestowed on a far less moral hero, whom at the time all classes delighted to honour:

> "Sancte Pater Patriæ, tibi plebs, tibi curia nomen
> Hoc dedit, hoc dedimus nos tibi nomen eques." [1]

---

[1] "Holy Father of thy Country! This title the Senates and the Commons, this title we, the Knights, have conferred on thee." (*Addressed to the Emperor Augustus.*)

APPENDIX

✦

ANOTHER TALK WITH MR. GLADSTONE—[1]

Qui genus humanum eloquio superavit.
LUCRETIUS (adapted).

A GREAT and well-merited interest is aroused by
everything that relates to Mr. Gladstone, and
especially by everything that throws light on his
social converse about which so little is known.
Bearing this in mind, I will take a further step
on the Boswellian track, shutting my ears to the
murmurs, fortunately only few and feeble, of disapproval which have assailed me. In cases of this
sort, newspapers do not always foreshadow the final
verdict of public opinion, and (if I may coin such
a word) the *Zeitunggeist* is not equivalent to the
Zeitgeist. To Boswellise a great man is an act
which some would wish not to be done, but which
all will one day rejoice to have been done.

This time, however, I am merely what may be
termed a proxy-Boswell. An accomplished divine,
who lives in France, and who saw a good deal of his
and my lamented friend at Biarritz, favoured me

<hr>

[1] Reprinted from *Literature*, August 20, 1898.

182

with two letters of reminiscence.   The second of these
letters is published in my "Talks with Mr. Gladstone" (pp. 93–97).   The other letter, written in the
previous year, was mislaid when I wrote my volume.
I have lately recovered it, and find, on reperusing
it, that it contains, along with some matter which
would be now out of date, a good deal which seems
likely to interest my readers.   With a few slight
and quasi-editorial corrections, I here transcribe the
important parts of that letter :—

Palmer's *Book of the Church* was a work the value of which, in
Mr. Gladstone's opinion, had not been sufficiently recognised.   It
had been much admired on the Continent.   Cardinal Perrone at
Rome had spoken to him about it, and said, "Oh that Palmer were
one of us !"   Döllinger also highly commended it, and wished that
a new edition should be made, bringing it down to date with matter
that had been discovered since it was first written.

Mr. Gladstone spoke of the many noble minds that he had met
among Roman Catholics—Lord Acton, Montalembert, and others.
One of them, who deplored much that was going on, believed that
even a reforming Pope of genius, like Hildebrand or Innocent III.,
could not effect anything, and added that there was no hope now
from Leo XIII.

Mr. Gladstone had known Cardinal Manning for many years.
He was difficult to understand, but there was a great deal of good
in him.

He spoke of Döllinger's vast learning, and of the Old Catholic
movement, and seemed surprised that it did not make more way
Père Hyacinthe's marriage was a mistake, deplored at the time by
friends, and even by French Protestants.   The Old Catholics had
acted more nobly, saying that those who were bound by vows should
remain so, but that all others were free.

He talked of Lamennais' genius, of Lacordaire, Montalembert,
and the Radical Ultramontane school, and of the Comte de Mun.
He agreed with me that it was the Ultramontane school which had
killed Gallicanism.

He spoke in a bitter tone of the English Roman Catholic peers. After all that the Liberal party had done for them, out of some thirty peers only two or three, Lord Ripon and others, were on what he held to be the right side.

I mentioned that it had taken me some years' residence abroad before I understood what foreigners meant by the *insularité* of the English mind and especially of the English clergy ; but that, now that I saw it, I could not look at things from the purely English point of view. I instanced all the histories of the Tractarian movement which we had had lately, including even Dean Church's ; all treated it as if it were a movement of English individuals ; not one of them connected it with the strictly parallel movement in France and elsewhere. But I did not convince him at all. He asked why had the English movement purified and improved the Church, while the corresponding Roman Catholic movement had almost the contrary effect. I suggested that the revival was real in Catholic countries ; but that the English Church had the safety valve of the too ardent spirits going to Rome ; whereas from Rome there was nowhere for such spirits to go to ; perforce they were kept seething within her. Again I did not win his assent.

He spoke of Butler's idea of nations going mad, and quoted the whole passage *verbatim.* I suggested that the solution was to be found in the existence of a real Personality of Evil and its struggles with the Good. He said that he believed most fully in a Personality of Evil.

He was convinced that there had been a very great improvement in the English clergy in devotion to their work ; still there were things that he might wish otherwise ; but, whereas formerly the indifferent were in the majority, now they were in the minority ; indeed, it was hard to find men wholly indifferent. The disestablishment of the Church, he thought, had retreated for the present— the clergy, through their devotion, had gained so much ground.

A high Catholic authority had told a friend of his that there was not *assez de foi* among the French clergy to make a revolution. [Renan likewise said of his countrymen that nowadays they are not religious enough to start a new heresy. He evidently regarded their character as having more in common with the sceptical acquiescence of Ecclesiastes than with the defiant blasphemy of Job, which latter he pronounced to be the mark of a more religious frame of mind.— L. A. T.]

Mr. Gladstone gave me (*à propos* of nothing in the conversation) a long account of Bernadino Ochino, the Italian Reformer, of his extraordinary eloquence, his career, his residence in Geneva, his going to Poland. In short, he gave a complete memoir of him in perfect style, so that it might have been reported word for word. But I could not make out what part of Ochino's life aroused Mr. Gladstone's sympathies, unless it were merely his coming out from Rome.

He spoke with intense admiration of the extraordinary intellect and brain power of Napoleon, as instanced in Marbot's *Memoirs*, of his wonderful grasp of details of all kinds, of his never losing himself in those details, and of his capacity of fitting each of them into its proper place in his general strategy and rule.

Boulanger, he said, was the worst political adventurer whom he had ever known. He had not even talent.

I was very much struck with the persuasive tone of Mr. Gladstone's voice and manner, which was distinctly that of one practised in the art of winning men. He was not dictatorial, nor had he the note of one accustomed to command, or to be listened to. The only departure from this tone was in his comment on the Roman Catholic peers, when there was a flash of bitter indignation, and in his long quotations from Butler and also in his improvisation on Ochino— then his tone became that which the French call the tone of one *qui s'écoute*.

On the whole, Mr. Gladstone gave me the impression of being a truly religious man ; it seemed to me that his intellect and inner thoughts were guided by theological ideas ; but that his outer conduct would be moulded almost entirely by political ones.

This discerning eulogy reminds me of the half playful tribute of praise which, some forty years ago, was paid to Mr. Gladstone when he was at Oxford canvassing the University electors. "Oh! Mr. Gladstone," said Max Müller, "why did you take up politics? *You were born to be a scholar!*" The significance of this latter compliment may haply be set in a stronger light by means of a

somewhat grotesque contrast. Such a contrast is
to be found in the Malapropism, or rather Dun-
drearyism, of the late eccentric Lord C——, who,
when speaking some years ago to Mrs. Gladstone,
said in a hesitating voice, as if fearful of over-
stating the fact, " I *think* that your husband takes
a great interest in politics." This unconscious
meiosis sounds too extravagant to be authentic;
but authentic it certainly is.

The combination in Mr. Gladstone of a strong
theological bias with great political sagacity was, at
least before people grew accustomed to it, a puzzle
and a stumbling-block to many able men. An
old-world incident may make my meaning clear.
Gladstone, Sir Roundell Palmer, and the Duke of
Argyle were seen at a London party, absorbed in
earnest conversation. Hayward went up and spoke
to them, or at anyrate passed within earshot. As
he withdrew, he encountered Delane, the then
Editor of *The Times*, who accosted him impatiently,
" What on earth are those three men talking about
all this time?" " They are discussing a new theological book called *Ecce Homo*." " If you don't
wish to tell me," exclaimed the incensed editor, " say
so frankly; but don't put me off with such damned
nonsense as that."

Mr. Gladstone once remarked in conversation that
Bright was fortunate in having lived to conciliate
his old enemies. Gladstone himself never achieved
this happy result, or achieved it only during his
last illness through the deep sympathy that was

felt for his prolonged suffering and through the world-wide admiration for his fortitude. But, on the other hand, he had the satisfaction of inspiring not a few of his innumerable followers with an almost filial regard. We often hear of men who have what is called "popular talent." Mr. Gladstone had popular genius. When he was speaking, his enthusiasm of humanity was so conspicuous in his face and voice, as well as in his words, that it became infectious; his exaltation lifted his hearers out of themselves. The result was that, in the view of many of his admirers, he became a sort of prematurely canonised saint (*præsens divus habebatur*). And perhaps even the most extravagant forms of hero-worship of which he was the object may have an interest as serving to explain, if not as warranting, the more moderate and reasonable forms. Two instances of such extravagance may be worth quoting. The first of these has reference to the agitation for the Disestablishment of the Welsh Church. Some time ago, a Welsh Nonconformist farmer inquired of his minister: "Isn't it the Holy Ghost that inspires Mr. Gladstone with those beautiful thoughts?" The other and more singular example bears quite a recent date. I am assured that a pious Gladstonian lady, on hearing the sad news of her hero's death, took comfort from the thought that his sphere of usefulness could not be closed: "for the Almighty will be certain to avail Himself of his valuable advice." It is easy to make fun of her edifying anthropomorphism, or

rather of her unconscious profanity—a profanity
suggestive of Shelley's description of Moses as the
"confidant of the All-knowing One." But perhaps,
after all, the admiration felt for Mr. Gladstone by
many female enthusiasts, if it were only writ large
and writ plain, would bear some resemblance to the
devotion of the good lady aforesaid. Mrs. Norton
maintained that all women in their hearts are believers in prayers for the dead. It might be added
as a corollary that the belief in the intercession of
the righteous dead for the living, nay, in their
helpful co-operation with the living, has a greater
hold on the female heart than most women would
acknowledge even to themselves. Well, be it so.
Wen Gott betrügt ist wohl betrogen.

MR. G.

APPENDIX I

A TOLLEMACHE DIALOGUE WITH JOWETT

May 7, 1893. — Jowett said that England seemed to him to run great risk of an invasion in the next fifty years; he thought there might be peril from Russia.

T. — 'Is not Russia weakened by Nihilism?'

J. — 'Not so much by Nihilism as by corruption. But even so, the mass would obey the Czar. He will in a few years be able to put five million in the field.'

T. — 'That is like Xerxes.'

J. — 'Yes, but they will be very different men from the Persians.'

T. — 'Shall not we be supported by Germany, Austria, and Italy?' He seemed doubtful about Austria and Italy. He spoke of China as another source of danger to Western civilisation, adding that, with its vast numbers and indifference to life, it has the making of a great military power.

We spoke of the recently-published *Life of Lord Sherbrooke* [Lowe], to which both he and I had contributed reminiscences.

J. — 'Lowe was in reality a thorough Liberal to the last.'

T. — 'Not, surely, a democratic Liberal!'

J. — 'No, but a philosophical Liberal. He had been on bad terms with the clergy, and was to the last anti-ecclesiastical.' He went on to intimate that Lowe was not wholly in the wrong; all history shows that religions become corrupt if they cease to keep terms with morality; if we are to tolerate the Church, she must be tolerant.

T. — 'Have not Evolution and Biblical Criticism thrown the Church on the defensive, and made her more tolerant than she ever was before?'

J. — 'Look at the damnatory clauses in the Athanasian Creed. If the clergyman who repeats them regards them as a mere dead letter, his conduct is not favourable to a high morality. If he believes in them, he imputes to God a very low morality.'

T. — 'I tell my American friends that when they discard the damnatory clauses they imply that the rest of the Creed is to be taken literally; and that thus, in the true sense of the saying, they make the *exception prove the rule*.'

J. — 'I would give up the Creed altogether.'

T. — 'Then would you not imply that the Apostles' and the Nicene Creeds are to be taken literally?'

J. — 'Every Church or Dissenting body must use compromise a little.'

T. — 'People call the Broad Church clergy dishonest. But they praise Marcus Aurelius up to the skies. And yet did not he, the Pontifex Maximus, the Pope of Paganism, practise conformity as completely as any Broad Church clergyman does now?' Jowett assented, but pointed out that, on the other hand, some philosophers tried to spiritualise Paganism; and this he considered the nobler course. He quoted the example of Socrates. I remarked that Socrates poured a libation to the Sun, and vowed a cock to Æsculapius. Not only did he thus cause the death of the poor little cock, but he implied that Æsculapius took pleasure in its sacrifice. This was giving countenance to vulgar superstition.

J. — 'Yes, I suppose this might be called an eccentricity. Perhaps he would not have much liked to be cross-questioned as to why he did it.' I hinted that he might have thought, as many Broad Churchmen now think, that a certain alloy of supernaturalism is the only way in which spiritual truths can be made to pass as current coin among the masses; or (to vary the metaphor) spiritual food should be not raw, but cooked for the infirm digestions of the multitude.

J. — 'I think that in the present day a religion without miracles would suit many people better than a religion with miracles.' I hinted that he was falling back on the theology of James Martineau, and that this stronghold is commonly thought to be not impregnable. It is open to attack from the disciples of Butler. If there is so much evil in the scheme of Nature, why not in that of Revelation? If in this life, why not in the next?

J. — 'This seems to me to be taking the question entirely at the wrong end.' I wished to cross-question him, but I was not sure whether he was not thinking of himself when he said that Socrates would not have liked to be cross-questioned. I therefore restrained the impulse; and especially I avoided expressing surprise that a severe criticism on the practice of economy of truth should have proceeded from an ultra Broad Church clergyman – from one, that is, who in his official character had to be practising economy of truth continually.

APPENDIX II

GLADSTONE IN OXFORD:
TALKS AT ALL SOULS COLLEGE

G. — 'I view with the greatest alarm the progress of Socialism of the present day.'

H.H.H. — 'Mr G., it lies with you to give it a great impulse forward or backward.'

G. — 'Whatever influence I can use, Mr H., will be used in the direction of stopping it. It will not be in my day, but it is alarming. It is the upper classes who are largely responsible for it.'

[Who is he thinking of?]

He ate everything. He drank, perfectly unconscious of what he was drinking, the first wine that came round to him. I thus noticed him drinking severally port, claret ... and brown sherry. He talked incessantly from seven-thirty till ten-twenty ...

With regard to Socialism, T.R. notes that he said further: 'For me, Socialism has no attractions: nothing but disappointment awaits the working classes if they yield to the exaggerated anticipations which are held out to them by the Labour Party.'

H.H.H. adds: 'He also expressed himself very positively on the subject of the greater class selfishness of the upper classes compared with the lower. I asked him whether Christianity was, in his opinion, as great a force in English politics as it was fifty years ago. He said, in reply, that he thought it was greater, though the manner of its expression had changed ...

When someone 'drew' him on the question of Church schools, it was, he told us, in this dual capacity that he 'regarded the Board School as a most unsatisfactory solution of the problem of popular education.'

To this A.H.H.: — 'I remember his rather staggering me by observing that the Duke of Wellington was quite right when he said in 1830 that the Constitution was incapable of improvement, and by his defending the saying on the ground that the contrast with the House of Lords exercised by means of the pocket boroughs over the House of Commons, established an ideal as well as a real equilibrium between the component parts of Parliament. He went on to say that the Reform Bill of 1832 destroyed this equilibrium, and that henceforward the Constitution was logically bound to develop on purely democratic lines, a result which he seemed to regard as a doubtful blessing.'

He also told C.G.L. outright that 'in point of ability and efficiency he thought the country had never been better governed than in the period preceding the First Reform Bill.'

APPENDIX III

MORLEY/GLADSTONE DIALOGUES AT BIARRITZ

We left Paris at nine in the morning [16 December 1891], and were listening to the swell of the mighty bay resounding under our windows at Biarritz soon after midnight.

The long day's journey left no signs of fatigue on either Mr or Mrs Gladstone, and his only regret was that we had not come straight through instead of staying a night in Paris. I'm always for going straight on, he said. For some odd reason in spite of the late hour he was full of stories of American humour, which he told with extraordinary verve and enjoyment. I contributed one that amused him much, of the Bostonian who, having read Shakespeare for the first time, observed, 'I call that a very clever book. Now, I don't suppose there are twenty men in Boston to-day who could have written that book!'

Thursday, December 17. — Splendid morning for making acquaintance with a new place. Saw the western spur of the Pyrenees falling down to the Bidassoa and the first glimpse of the giant wall, beyond which, according to Michelet, Africa begins, and our first glimpse of Spain.

After breakfast we all sallied forth to look into the shops and to see the lie of the land. Mr G as interested as a child in all the objects in the shops – many of them showing that we are not far from Spain ...

Some mention was made of Charles Austin, the famous lawyer: it brought up the case of men who are suddenly torn from lives of great activity to complete idleness.

Mr G. — 'I don't know how to reconcile it with what I've always regarded as the foundation of character – Bishop Butler's view of habit. How comes it that during the hundreds of years in which priests and fellows of Eton College have retired from hard work to College livings and leisure, not one of them has ever done anything whatever for either scholarship or divinity – not one?'

Mr G. did not know Mazzini, but Armellini, another of the Roman triumvirs, taught him Italian in 1832.

I spoke a word for Gambetta, but he would not have it. 'Gambetta was *autoritaire*; I do not feel as if he were a true liberal in the old and best sense. I cannot forget how hostile he was to the movement for freedom in the Balkans.'

Said he only once saw Lord Liverpool. He went to call on Canning at Glos'ter House (close to our Glos'ter Road Station), and there through a glass door he saw Canning and Lord Liverpool talking together.

Peel. — 'Had a good deal of temper; not hot; but perhaps sulky. Not a farsighted man, but fairly clear-sighted.' 'I called upon him after the election in 1847. The Janissaries, as Bentinck called us, that is the men who had stood by Peel, had been 110 before the election; we came back only 50. Peel said to me that what he looked forward to was a long and fierce struggle on behalf of Protection. I must say I thought this foolish. If Bentinck had lived, with his strong will and dogged industry, there might have been a wide rally for protection, but everybody knew that Dizzy did not care a straw about it, and Derby had not constancy and force enough.'

Mr G. said Disraeli's performances against Peel were quite as wonderful as report makes them. Peel altogether helpless in reply. Dealt with them with a kind of 'righteous dulness.' The Protectionist secession due to three men: Derby contributed prestige;Bentinck backbone; and Dizzy parliamentary brains.

The golden age of administrative reform was from 1832 to the Crimean War; Peel was always keenly interested in the progress of these reforms.

Northcote. — 'He was my private secretary; and one of the very best imaginable; pliant, ready, diligent, quick, acute, with plenty of humour, and a temper simply perfect. But as a leader, I think ill of him; you had a conversation; he saw the reason of your case; and when he left, you supposed all was right. But at the second interview, you always found that he had been unable to persuade his friends. What could be weaker than his conduct on the Bradlaugh affair! You could not wonder that the rank and file of his men should be caught by the proposition that an atheist ought not to sit in Parliament. But what is a leader good for, if he dare not tell his party that in a matter like this they are wrong, and of course nobody knew better than N. that they were wrong. A clever, quick man with fine temper. By the way, how is it that we have no word, no respectable word, for backbone?'

J.M. — 'Character?'

Mr G. — 'Well, character; yes; but that's vague. It means will, I suppose.' (I ought to have thought of Novalis's well-known definition of character as 'a completely fashioned will.')

J.M. — 'Our inferiority to the Greeks in discriminations of language shown by our lack of precise equivalents for $\phi\rho\acute{o}\nu\eta\sigma\iota\varsigma$, $\sigma o\phi\acute{\iota}a$, $\sigma\omega\phi\rho o\sigma\acute{\nu}\eta$, etc., of which we used to hear so much when coached in the *Ethics.*'

Mr G. went on to argue that because the Greeks drew these fine distinctions in words, they were superior in conduct. 'You cannot beat the Greeks in noble qualities.'

Mr G. — 'I admit there is no Greek word of good credit for the virtue of humility.'

J.M. — '$\tau a\pi\epsilon\iota\nu\acute{o}\tau\eta\varsigma$? But that has an association of meanness.'

Mr G. — 'Yes; a shabby sort of humility. Humility as a sovereign grace is the creation of Christianity.'

Friday, December 18. — Brilliant sunshine, but bitterly cold; an east wind blowing straight from the Maritime Alps. Walking, reading, talking. Mr G. after breakfast took me into his room, where he is reading Heine, Butcher on Greek genius, and Marbot. Thought Thiers's well-known remark on Heine's death capital, – 'Today the wittiest Frenchman alive has died.'

Mr G. — 'We have talked about the best line in poetry, etc. How do you answer this question – Which century of English history produced the greatest men?'

J.M. — 'What do you say to the sixteenth?'

Mr G. — 'Yes, I think so. Gardiner was a great man. Henry VIII was great. But bad. Poor Cranmer. Like Northcote, he'd no backbone. Do you remember Jeremy Collier's sentence about his bravery at the stake, which I count one of the grandest in English prose – "He seemed to repel the force of the fire and to overlook the torture, by strength of thought."[1] Thucydides could not beat that.'

The old man twice declaimed the sentence with deep sonorous voice, and his usual incomparable modulation.

Mr G. talked of a certain General —— . He was thought to be a first-rate man; neglected nothing, looked to things himself, conceived, admirable plans, and at last got an important command. Then to the universal surprise, nothing came of it; —— , they said, 'could do everything that a commander should do, except say, *Quick march.*' There are plenty of politicians of that stamp, but Mr G. decidedly not one of them. I mentioned a farewell dinner given to —— in the spring, by some rich man or other. It cost £560 for forty-eight guests! Flowers alone £150. Mr G. on this enormity, recalled a dinner to Talfourd about copyright at the old Clarendon Hotel in Bond Street, and the price was £2. 17s. 6d. a head. The old East India Company used to give dinners at a cost of seven guineas a head. He has a wonderfully lively interest for these matters, and his curiosity as to the prices of things in the shop-windows is inexhaustible. We got round to Goethe. Goethe, he said, never gave prominence to duty.

J.M. — 'Surely, surely in that fine psalm of life, *Das Göttliche?*'

Mr G. — 'Döllinger used to confront me with the *Iphigenie* as a great drama of duty.'

He wished that I had known Döllinger — 'a man thoroughly from beginning to end of his life *purged of self.*' Mistook the nature of the Irish questions, from the erroneous view that Irish Catholicism is Ultramontane, which it certainly is not.

Saturday, Dec. 19. —

What is extraordinary is that all Mr G.'s versatility, buoyancy, and the rest goes with the most profound accuracy and intense concentration when any point of public business is raised. Something was said of the salaries of bishops. He was ready in an instant with every figure and detail, and every circumstance of the history of the foundation of the Ecclesiastical Commission in 1835-6. Then his *savoir faire* and wisdom of parliamentary conduct. 'I always made it a rule in the H. of C. to allow nobody to suppose that I did not like him, and to say as little as I could to prevent anybody from liking me. Considering the intense friction and contention of public life, it is a saving of wear and tear that as many as possible even among opponents should think well of one.'

Sunday, Dec. 20. — At table, a little discussion as to the happiness and misery of animal creation. Outside of man Mr G. argued against Tennyson's description of Nature as red in tooth and claw. Apart from man, he said, and the action of man, sentient beings are happy and not miserable. But Fear? we said. No; they are unaware of impending doom; when hawk or kite pounces on its prey, the small bird has little or no apprehension; 'tis death, but death by appointed and unforeseen lot.

J.M. — 'There is Hunger. Is not the probability that most creatures are always hungry, not excepting Man?'

To this he rather assented. Of course optimism like this is indispensable as the basis of natural theology.

Talked to Mr G. about Michelet's *Tableau de la France*, which I had just finished in vol. 2 of the history. A brilliant *tour de force*, but strains the relations of soil to character; compels words and facts to be the slaves of his phantasy; the modicum of reality overlaid with violent paradox and foregone conclusion. Mr G. not very much interested – seems only to care for political and church history.

Monday, Dec. 21. — Mr G. did not appear at table today, suffering from a surfeit of wild strawberries the day before. But he dined in his dressing-gown, and I had some chat with him in his room after lunch.

Mr G. — ''Tis a hard law of political things that if a man shows special competence in a department, that is the very thing most likely to keep him there, and prevent his promotion.'

Mr G. — 'I consider Burke a tripartite man: America, France, Ireland — right as to two, wrong in one.'

J.M. — 'Must you not add home affairs and India? His *Thoughts on the Discontents* is a masterpiece of civil wisdom, and the right defence in a great constitutional struggle. Then he gave fourteen years of industry to Warren Hastings, and teaching England the rights of the natives, princes and people, and her own duties. So he was right in four out of five.'

Mr G. — 'Yes, yes – quite true. Those two ought to be added to my three. There is a saying of Burke's from which I must utterly dissent. "Property is sluggish and inert." Quite the contrary. Property is vigilant, active, sleepless; if ever it seems to slumber, be sure that one eye is open.'

Marie Antoinette. — I once read the three volumes of letters from Mercy d'Argenteau to Maria Theresa. He seems to have performed the duty imposed upon him with fidelity.

J.M. — 'Don't you think the Empress comes out well in the correspondence?'

Mr G. — 'Yes, she shows always judgment and sagacity.'

J.M. — 'Ah, but besides sagacity, worth and as much integrity as those slippery times allowed.'

Mr G. — 'Yes.' (*But rather reluctantly, I thought.*) 'As for Marie Antoinette, she was not a striking character in any sense; she was horribly frivolous; and, I suppose, we must say she was, what shall I call it — a very considerable flirt?' ....

Tuesday, Dec. 22. — Mr G. still somewhat indisposed – but reading away all day long.....

Talk about the dangerous isolation in which the monarchy will find itself in England if the hereditary principle goes down in the House of Lords; 'it will stand bare, naked, with no shelter or shield, only endured as the better of two evils.' 'I once asked,' he said, 'who besides myself in the party cares for the hereditary principle? The answer was, That perhaps —— cared for it!!' – naming a member of the party supposed to be rather sapient than sage.

News in the paper that the Comte de Paris in his discouragement was about to renounce his claims, and break up his party. Somehow this brought us round to de Tocqueville, of whom Mr G. spoke as the nearest French approach to Burke.

J.M. — 'But pale and without passion. Who was it that said of him that he was an aristocrat who accepted his defeat? That is, he knew democracy to be the conqueror, but he doubted how far it would be an improvement, he saw its perils, etc.'

Mr G. — 'I have not much faith in these estimates, whether in favour of progress or against it. I don't believe in comparisons of age with age. How can a man strike a balance between one Government and another? How can he place himself in such an attitude, and with such comprehensive sureness of vision, as to say that the thirteenth century was better or higher or worse or lower than the nineteenth?'

Thursday, Dec. 24. — At lunch we had the news of the Parnellite victory at Waterford. A disagreeable reverse for us. Mr G. did not say many words about it, only that it would give heart to the mischief makers – only too certain. But we said no more about it. He and I took a walk on the sands in the afternoon, and had a curious talk (considering), about the prospects of the Church of England. He was anxious to know about my talk some time ago with the Bishop of —— whom I had met at a feast at Lincoln's Inn. I gave him as good an account as I could of what had passed. Mr G. doubted that this prelate was fundamentally an Erastian, as Tait was. Mr G. is eager to read the signs of the times as to the prospects of anglican Christianity, to which his heart is given; and he fears the peril of Erastianism to the spiritual life of the Church, which is naturally the only thing worth caring about. Hence, he talked with much interest of the question whether the clever Fellows at Oxford and Cambridge now take Orders. He wants to know what kind of defenders his Church is likely to have in days to come. Said that for the first time interest has moved away both from politics and theology, towards the vague something which they call social reform; and he thinks they won't make much out of that in the way of permanent results. The establishment he considers safer than it has been for a long time.

As to Welsh disestablishment, he said it was a pity that where the national sentiment was so unanimous as it was in Wales, the operation itself should not be as simple as in Scotland. In Scotland sentiment is not unanimous, but the operation is easy. In Wales sentiment is all one way, but the operation difficult – a good deal more difficult than people suppose, as they will find out when they come to tackle it.

(Perhaps it may be mentioned here that, though we always talked freely and abundantly together upon ecclesiastical affairs and persons, we never once exchanged a word upon theology or religious creed, either at Biarritz or anywhere else.)

Pitt. — A strong denunciation of Pitt for the French war. People don't realise what the French war meant. In 1812 wheat at Liverpool was 20s. [?] the imperial bushel of 65 pounds [?]! Think of that, when you bring it into figures of the cost of a loaf. And that was the time when Eaton, Eastnor, and other great palaces were built by the landlords off the high rents which the war and war prices enabled them to exact.

Wished we knew more of Melbourne. He was in many ways a very fine fellow. 'In two of the most important of all the relations of a Prime Minister, he was perfect; I mean first, his relations to the Queen, second to his colleagues.'

Somebody at dinner quoted a capital description of the perverse fashion of talking that prevailed at Oxford soon after my time, and prevails there now, I fancy – hunting for epigrammatic ways of saying what you don't think. —— was the father of this pestilent mode.

Rather puzzled him by repeating a saying of mine that used to amuse Fitzjames Stephen, that Love of Truth is more often than we think only a fine name for Temper. I think Mr G. has a thorough dislike for anything that has a cynical or sardonic flavour about it. . . . .

Am always feeling how strong is his aversion to seeing more than he can help of what is sordid, mean, ignoble. He has not been in public life all these years without rubbing shoulders with plenty of baseness on every scale, and plenty of pettiness in every hue, but he has always kept his eyes well above it. Never was a man more wholly free of the starch of the censor, more ready to make allowance, nor more indulgent even; he enters into human nature in all its compass. But he won't linger a minute longer than he must in the dingy places of life and character.

Christmas Day, 1891. — A divine day, brilliant sunshine, and mild spring air. Mr G. heard what he called an admirable sermon from an English preacher, 'with a great command of his art.' . . . .

Saturday, Dec. 26. — Once more a noble day. We started in a couple of carriages for the Négress station, a couple of miles away or more, I with the Gs. Occasion produced the Greek epitaph of the nameless drowned sailor who wished for others kinder seas.[2] Mr G. felt its pathos and its noble charm – so direct and simple, such benignity, such a good lesson to men to forget their own misdeeds and mischance, and to pray for the passer-by a happier star. He repaid me by two epigrams of a different vein, and one admirable translation into Greek, of Tennyson on Sir John Franklin, which I do not carry in my mind; another on a boisterous Eton fellow –

> Didactic, dry, declamatory, dull,
> The bursar —— bellows like a bull.

Just in the tone of Greek epigram, a sort of point, but not too much point.

Parliamentary Wit. — Thought Disraeli had never been surpassed, nor even equalled, in this line. he had a contest with General Grey, who stood upon the general merits of the Whig Government, after both Lord Grey and Stanley had left it. D. drew a picture of a circus man who advertised his show with its incomparable team of six grey horses. One died, he replaced it by a mule. Another died, and he put in a donkey, still he went on advertising his team of greys all the same. Canning's wit not to be found conspicuously in his speeches, but highly agreeable pleasantries, though many of them in a vein which would jar horribly on modern taste.

Some English Redcoats and a pack of hounds passed us as we neared the station. They saluted Mr G. with a politeness that astonished him, but was pleasant. Took the train for Irun, the fields and mountain slopes delightful in the sun, and the sea on our right a superb blue such as we never see in English waters. At Irun we found carriages waiting to take us on to Fuentarabia. From the balcony of the church had a beautiful view over the scene of Wellington's operations when he crossed the Bidassoa, in the presence of the astonished Soult. A lovely picture, made none the worse by this excellent historic association. . . .

Pretty cold driving home, but Mr G. seemed not to care. . . .

Sunday, Dec. 27. — After some quarter of an hour of travellers' topics, we plunged into one of the most interesting talks we have yet had. *Apropos* of I do not know what, Mr G. said that he had not advised his son to enter public life. 'No doubt there are some men to whom station, wealth, and family traditions make it a duty. But I have never advised any individual, as to whom I have been consulted, to enter the H. of C.'

J.M. — 'But isn't that rather to encourage self-indulgence? Nobody who cares for ease or mental composure would seek public life?

Mr G. — 'Ah, I don't know that. Surely politics open up a great field for the natural man. Self-seeking pride, domination, power — all these passions are gratified in politics.'

J.M. — 'You cannot be sure of achievement in politics, whether personal or public?

Mr G. — 'No; to use Bacon's pregnant phrase, they are too immersed in matter. Then as new matter, that is, new details and particulars, come into view, men change their judgment.'

J.M. — 'You have spoken just now of somebody as a thorough good Tory. You know the saying that nobody is worth much who has not been a bit of a radical in his youth, and a bit of a tory in his fuller age.'

Mr G. (laughing) — 'Ah, I'm afraid that hits me rather hard. But for myself, I think I can truly put up all the change that has come into my politics into a sentence; I was brought up to distrust and dislike liberty, I learned to believe in it. That is the key to all my changes.'

J.M. — 'According to my observations, the change in my own generation is different. They have ceased either to trust or to distrust liberty, and have come to the mind that it matters little either way. Men are disenchanted. They have got what they wanted in the days of their youth, yet what of it, they ask? France has thrown off the Empire, but the statesmen of the republic are not a great breed. Italy has gained her unity, yet unity has not been followed by thrift, wisdom, or large increase of public virtue or happiness. America has purged herself of slavery, yet life in America is material, prosaic, – so say some of her own rarest sons. Don't think that I say all these things. But I know able and high-minded men who suffer from this disenchantment.'

Mr G. — 'Italy would have been very different if Cavour had only lived – and even Ricasoli. Men ought not to suffer from disenchantment. They ought to know that *ideals in politics are never realised*. And don't let us forget in eastern Europe the rescue in our time of some ten millions of men from the harrowing domination of the Turk.' (On this he expatiated, and very justly, with much energy.)

We turned to our own country. Here he insisted that Democracy had certainly not saved us from a distinct decline in the standard of public men.... Look at the whole conduct of opposition from '80 to '85 – every principle was flung overboard, if they could manufacture a combination against the government. For all this deterioration one man and one man alone is responsible, Disraeli. He is the grand corrupter. He it was who sowed the seed.

J.M. — 'Ought not Palmerston to bear some share in this?'

Mr G. — 'No, no; Pam. had many strong and liberal convictions. On one subject Dizzy had them too – the Jews. There he was much more than rational, he was fanatical. He said once that Providence would deal good or ill-fortune to nations, according as they dealt well or ill by the Jews. I remember once sitting next to John Russell when D. was making a speech on Jewish emancipation. 'Look at him,' said J.R., 'how manfully he sticks to it, tho' he knows that every word he says is gall and wormwood to every man who sits around him and behind him.' A curious irony, was it not, that it should have fallen to me to propose a motion for a memorial both to Pam. and Dizzy?'

A superb scene upon the ocean, with a grand wind from the west. Mr G. and I walked on the shore; he has a passion for tumultuous seas. I have never seen such huge masses of water, shattering themselves among the rocks.

In the evening Mr G. remarked on our debt to Macaulay, for guarding the purity of the English tongue. I recalled a favourite passage from Milton, that next to the man who gives wise and intrepid counsels of government, he places the man who cares for the purity of his mother tongue. Mr G. liked this. Said he only knew Bright once slip into an error in this respect, when he used 'transpire' for 'happen.' Macaulay of good example also in rigorously abstaining from the inclusion of matter in footnotes. Hallam an offender in this respect. I pointed out that he offended in company with Gibbon.

Monday, Dec. 28. — We had an animated hour at breakfast.
Oxford and Cambridge. — Curious how, like two buckets, whenever one was up, the other was down. Cambridge has never produced four such men of action in successive ages as Wolsey, Laud, Wesley, and Newman.

J.M. — 'In the region of thought Cambridge has produced the greatest of all names, Newton.'

Mr G. — 'In the earlier times Oxford has it – with Wycliff, Occam, above all Roger Bacon. And then in the eighteenth century, Butler.'

J.M. — 'But why not Locke, too, in the century before?'

This brought on a tremendous tussle, for Mr G. was of the same mind, and perhaps for the same sort of reason, as Joseph de Maistre, that contempt for Locke is the beginning of knowledge. All very well for De Maistre, but not for a man in line with European Liberalism. I pressed the very obvious point that you must take into account not only a man's intellectual product or his general stature, but also his influence as a historic force. From the point of view of influence Locke was the origin of the emancipatory movement of the eighteenth century abroad, and laid the philosophic foundations of liberalism in civil government at home. Mr G. insisted on a passage of Hume's which he believed to be in the history, disparaging Locke as a metaphysical thinker.[3] 'That may be,' said I, 'though Hume in his *Essays* is not above paying many compliments to "the great reasoner," etc., to whom for that matter, I fancy that he stood in pretty direct relation. But far be it from me to deny that Hume saw deeper than Locke into the metaphysical millstone. That is not the point. I'm only thinking of his historic place, and after all, the history of philosophy is itself a philosophy.' To minds nursed in dogmatic schools, all this is both unpalatable and incredible.

Somehow we slid into the freedom of the will and Jonathan Edwards. I told him that Mill had often told us how Edwards argued the necessarian or determinist case as keenly as any modern.

Tuesday, Dec. 29. — Mr G. 82 to-day. I gave him Mackail's *Greek Epigrams*, and if it affords him half as much pleasure as it has given me, he will be very grateful. Various people brought Mr G. bouquets and addresses. Mr G. went to church in the morning, and in the afternoon took a walk with me . . . . *Land Question.* As you go through France you see the soil cultivated by the population. In our little dash into Spain the other day, we saw again the soil cultivated by the population. In England it is cultivated by the capitalist, for the farmer is capitalist. Some astonishing views recently propounded by D. of Argyll on this matter. Unearned increment – so terribly difficult to catch it. Perhaps best try to get at it through the death duties. Physical condition of our people – always a subject of great anxiety – their stature, colour, and so on. Feared the atmosphere of cotton factories, etc., very deleterious. As against bad air, I said, you must set good food; the Lancashire operative in decent times lives uncommonly well, as he deserves to do. He agreed there might be something in this.

The day was humid and muggy, but the tumult of the sea was most majestic. Mr G. delighted in it. He has a passion for the sound of the sea; would like to have it in his ear all day and all night. Again and again he recurred to this.

After dinner, long talk about Mazzini, of whom Mr G. thought poorly in comparison with Poerio and the others who for freedom sacrificed their lives. I stood up for Mazzini, as one of the most morally impressive men I had ever known, or that his age knew; he breathed a soul into democracy.

Then we fell into a discussion as to the Eastern and Western Churches. He thought the Western popes by their proffered alliance with the Mahometans, etc., had betrayed Christianity in the East. I offered De Maistre's view.

Mr G. strongly assented to old Chatham's dictum that vacancy is worse than even the most anxious work. He has less to reproach himself with than most men under that head.

He repeated an observation that I have heard him make before, that he thought politicians are more *rapid* than other people. I told him that Bowen once said to me on this that he did not agree; that he thought rapidity the mark of all successful men in the practical line of life, merchants and stockbrokers, etc.

Wednesday, Dec. 30. — A very muggy day. A divine sunset, with the loveliest pink and opal tints in the sky. Mr G. reading Gleig's *Subaltern.* Not a very entertaining book in itself, but the incidents belong to Wellington's Pyrenean campaign, and, for my own part, I rather enjoyed it on the principle on which one likes reading *Romola* at Florence, *Transformation* at Rome, *Sylvia's Lovers* at Whitby, and *Hurrish* on the northern edge of Clare.

Thursday, Dec. 31. — Down to the pier, and found all the party watching the breakers, and superb they were. Mr G. exulting in the huge force of the Atlantic swell and the beat of the rollers on the shore, like a Titanic pulse.

After dinner Mr G. raised the question of payment of members. He had been asked by somebody whether he meant at Newcastle to indicate that everybody should be paid, or only those who chose to take it or to ask for it. He produced the same extraordinary plan as he had described to me on the morning of his Newcastle speech – i.e. that the Inland Revenue should ascertain from their own books the income of every MP, and if they found any below the limit of exemption, should notify the same to the Speaker, and the Speaker should thereupon send to the said MP below the limit an annual cheque for, say, £300, the name to appear in an annual return to Parliament of all the MPs in receipt of public money on any grounds whatever. I demurred to this altogether, as drawing an invidious distinction between paid and unpaid members; said it was idle to ignore the theory on which the demand for paid members is based, namely, that it is desirable in the public interest that poor men should have access to the H. of C.; and that the poor man should stand there on the same footing as anybody else.

Friday, Jan. 1, 1892. — After breakfast Mrs Gladstone came to my room and said how glad she was that I had not scrupled to put unpleasant points; that Mr G. must not be shielded and sheltered as some great people are, who hear all the pleasant things and none of the unpleasant; that the perturbation from what is disagreeable only lasts an hour. I said I hoped that I was faithful with him, but of course I could not be always putting myself in an attitude of perpetual controversy. She said, 'He is never made angry by what you say.' And so she went away, and —— and I had a good and most useful set-to about Irish finance.

At luncheon Mr G. asked what we had made out of our morning's work. When we told him, he showed a good deal of impatience and vehemence, and, to my dismay, he came upon Union finance and the general subject of the treatment of Ireland by England....

In the afternoon we took a walk, he and I, afterwards joined by the rest. he was as delighted as ever with the swell of the waves, as they bounded over one another, with every variety of grace and tumultuous power. he wondered if we had not more and better words for the sea than the French – 'breaker,' 'billow,' 'roller,' as against *'flot,' 'vague,' 'onde,' 'lame,'* etc.

At dinner he asked me whether I had made up my mind on the burning question of compulsory Greek for a university degree. I said, No, that as then advised I was half-inclined to be against compulsory Greek, but it is so important that I would not decide before I was obliged. 'So with me,' he said, 'the question is one with many subtle and deep-reaching consequences.' He dwelt on the folly of striking Italian out of the course of modern education, thus cutting European history in two, and setting an artificial gap between the ancient and modern worlds.

Saturday, Jan. 2. — Superb morning, and all the better for being much cooler. At breakfast somebody started the idle topic of quill pens. When they came to the length of time that so-and-so made a quill serve, 'De Retz,' said I, 'made up his mind that Cardinal Chigi was a poor creature, *maximus in minimis*, because at their first interview Chigi boasted that he had used one pen for three years.' That recalled another saying of Retz's about Cromwell's famous dictum, that nobody goes so far as the man who does not know where he is going. Mr G. gave his deep and eager Ah! to this. He could not recall that Cromwell had produced many dicta of such quality. 'I don't love him, but he was a mighty big fellow. But he was intolerant. He was intolerant of the Episcopalians.'

Mr G. — 'Do you know whom I find the most tolerant churchman of that time? *Laud!* Laud got Davenant made Bishop of Salisbury, and he zealously befriended Chillingworth and Hales.' (*There was some other case, which I forget.*)

The Execution of Charles. — I told him of Gardiner's new volume which I had just been reading. 'Charles,' he said, 'was no doubt a dreadful liar; Cromwell perhaps did not always tell the truth; Elizabeth was a tremendous liar.'

J.M. — 'Charles was not wholly inexcusable, being what he was, for thinking that he had a good game in his hands, by playing off the parliament against the army, etc.'

Mr G. — 'There was less excuse for cutting off his head than in the case of poor Louis XVI, for Louis was the excuse for foreign invasion.'

J.M. — 'Could you call foreign invasion the intervention of the Scotch?'

Mr G. — 'Well, not quite. I suppose it is certain that it was Cromwell who cut off Charles's head? Not one in a hundred in the nation desired it.'

J.M. — 'No, nor one in twenty in the Parliament. But then, ninety-nine in a hundred in the army.'

In the afternoon we all drove towards Bayonne to watch the ships struggle over the bar at high water. As it happened we only saw one pass out, a countryman for Cardiff. A string of others were waiting to go, but a little steamer from Nantes came first, and having secured her station, found she had not force enought to make the bar, and the others remained swearing impatiently behind her. The Nantes steamer was like Ireland. The scene was very fresh and fine, and the cold most exhilarating after the mugginess of the last two or three days. Mr G., who has a dizzy head, did not venture on the jetty, but watched things from the sands.

He and I drove home together, at a good pace. 'I am inclined,' he said laughingly, 'to agree with Dr Johnson that there is no pleasure greater than sitting behind four fast-going horses.' Talking of Johnson generally, 'I suppose we may take him as the best product of the eighteenth century.' Perhaps so, but is he its most characteristic product?

Wellington. — Curious that there should be no general estimate of W.'s character; his character not merely as a general but as a man. No love of freedom. His sense of duty very strong, but military rather than civil....

Latin Poets. — Would you place Virgil first?

J.M. — 'Oh, no, Lucretius much the first for the greatest and sublimest of poetic qualities. Mr G. seemed to assent to this, though disposed to make a fight for the second *Æneid* as equal to anything. He expressed his admiration for Catallus, and then he was strong that Horace would run anybody else very hard....

Blunders in Government. — How right Napoleon was when he said, reflecting on all the vast complexities of government, that the best to be said of a statesman is that he has avoided the biggest blunders.

It is not easy to define the charm of these conversations. Is charm the right word? They are in the highest degree stimulating, bracing, widening. That is certain. I return to my room with the sensations of a man who has taken delightful exercise in fresh air. He is so wholly free from the *ergoteur.* There's all the difference between the *ergoteur* and the great debater. He fits his tone to the thing; he can be as playful as anybody. In truth I have many a time seen him in London and at Hawarden not far from trivial. But here at Biarritz all is appropriate, and though, as I say, he can be playful and gay as youth, he cannot resist rising in an instant to the general point of view – to grasp the elemental considerations of character, history, belief, conduct, affairs. There he is at home, there he is most himself. I never knew anybody less guilty of the tiresome sin of arguing for victory. It is not his knowledge that attracts; it is not his ethical tests and standards; it is not that dialectical strength of arm which, as Mark Pattison said of him, could twist a bar of iron to its purpose. It is the combination of these with elevation, with true sincerity, with extraordinary mental force.

Sunday, Jan. 3. —....

At dinner he showed in full force.

Heroes of the Old Testament. — He could not honestly say that he thought there was any figure in the O.T. comparable to the heroes of Homer. Moses was a fine fellow. But the others were of secondary quality – not great high personages, of commanding nature.

Thinkers. — Rather an absurd word – to call a man a thinker (and he repeated the word with gay mockery in his tone). When did it come into use? Not until quite our own times, eh? I said, I believed both Hobbes and Locke spoke of thinkers, and was pretty sure that *penseur*, as in *libre penseur*, had established itself in the last century. (Quite true; Voltaire used it, but it was not common.)

Dr Arnold. — A high, large, impressive figure – perhaps more important by his character and personality than his actual work. I mentioned M.A.'s poem on his father, *Rugby Chapel*, with admiration. Rather to my surprise, Mr G. knew the poem well, and shared my admiration to the full. This brought us on to poetry generally, and he expatiated with much eloquence and sincerity for the rest of the talk. The wonderful continuity of fine poetry in England for five whole centuries, stretching from Chaucer to Tennyson, always a proof to his mind of the soundness, the sap, and the vitality of our nation and its character. What people, beginning with such a poet as Chaucer 500 years ago, could have burst forth into such astonishing production of poetry as marked the first quarter of the century, Byron, Wordworth, Shelley, etc.

J.M. — 'It is true that Germany has nothing, save Goethe, Schiller, Heine, that's her whole list.' But I should say a word for the poetic movement in France: Hugo, Gautier, etc. Mr G. evidently knew but little, or even nothing of modern French poetry. He spoke up for Leopardi, on whom he had written an article first introducing him to the British public, ever so many years ago – in the *Quarterly*.

Mr G. — 'Wordworth used occasionally to dine with me when I lived in the Albany. A most agreeable man. I always found him amiable, polite, and sympathetic. Only once did he jar upon me, when he spoke slightingly of Tennyson's first performance.'

J.M. — 'But he was not so wrong as he would be now. Tennyson's Juvenilia are terribly artificial.'

Mr G. — 'Yes, perhaps. Tennyson has himself withdrawn some of them. I remember W., when he dined with me, used on leaving to change his silk stockings in the ante-room and put on grey worsted.'

J.M. — 'I once said to M. Arnold that I'd rather have been Wordsworth than anybody [not exactly a modest ambition]; and Arnold, who knew him well in the Grasmere country, said, "Oh no, you would not; you would wish you were dining with me at the Athenæum. He was too much of the peasant for you."'

Mr G. — 'No, I never felt that; I always thought him a polite and an amiable man.'

Mentioned Macaulay's strange judgment in a note in the *History*, that Dryden's famous lines,

> '.. Fool'd with hope, men favour the deceit;
> Trust on, and think to-morrow will repay.
> To-morrow's falser than the former day;
> Lies worse, and while it says we shall be blest
> With some new joys, cuts off what we possest.
> Strange cozenage!' ...

are as fine as any eight lines in Lucretius. Told him of an excellent remark of ——
on this, that Dryden's passage wholly lacks the mystery and great superhuman air
of Lucretius. Mr G. warmly agreed.

He regards it as a remarkable sign of the closeness of the Church of England to
the roots of life and feeling in the country, that so many clergymen should have
written so much good poetry. Who, for instance? I asked. He named Heber,
Moultrie, Newman (*Dream of Gerontius*), and Faber in at least one good poem,
'The poor Labourer' (or some such title), Charles Tennyson. I doubt if this
thesis has much body in it. He was for Shelley as the most musical of all our poets.
I told him that I had once asked M. to get Tennyson to write an autograph line
for a friend of mine, and Tennyson had sent this: –
'Coldly on the dead volcano sleeps the gleam of dying day.'
So I suppose the poet must think well of it himself. 'Tis from the second *Locksley
Hall*, and describes a man after passions have gone cool.

Mr G. — 'Yes, in melody, in the picturesque, and as apt simile, a fine line.'

Had been trying his hand at a translation of his favourite lines of Penelope
about Odysseus. Said that, of course, you could translate similes and set
passages, but to translate Homer as a whole, impossible. He was inclined, when
all is said, to think Scott the nearest approach to a model.

Monday, Jan. 4. — At luncheon, Mr Gladstone recalled the well-known story of
Talleyrand on the death of Napoleon. The news was brought when T. chanced to
be dining with Wellington. 'Quel évènement!' they all cried. 'Non, ce n'est pas
un évènement,' said Talleyrand, 'c'est une nouvelle' – 'Tis no event, 'tis a piece of
news.' 'Imagine such a way,' said Mr G., 'of taking the disappearance of that
colossal man! Compare it with the opening of Manzoni's ode, which makes the
whole earth stand still. Yet both points of view are right. In one sense, the giant's
death was only news; in another, when we think of his history, it was enough to
shake the world.' At the moment, he could not recall Manzoni's words, but at
dinner he told me that he had succeeded in piecing them together, and after
dinner he went to his room and wrote them down for me on a piece of paper.
Curiously enough, he could not recall the passage in his own splendid translation.'[4]

Talk about handsome men of the past; Sidney Herbert one of the handsomest
and most attractive. But the Duke of Hamilton bore away the palm, as glorious
as a Greek god. 'One day in Rotten Row, I said this to the Duchess of C. She set
up James Hope-Scott against my Duke. No doube he had an intellectual element
which the Duke lacked.' Then we discussed the best-looking man in the H. of C.
today....

Duke of Wellington. — Somebody was expatiating on the incomparable position of the Duke; his popularity with kings, with nobles, with common people.
Mr G. remembered that immediately after the formation of Canning's Govern-

ment in 1827, when it was generally thought that he had been most unfairly and factiously treated (as Mr G. still thinks, always saving Peel) by the Duke and his friends, the Duke made an expedition to the north of England, and had an overwhelming reception. Of course, he was then only twelve years from Waterloo, and yet only four or five years later he had to put up his iron shutters.

Approved a remark that a friend of ours was not simple enough, not ready enough to take things as they come.

Mr G. — 'Unless a man has a considerable gift for taking things as they come, he may make up his mind that political life will be sheer torment to him. He must meet fortune in all its moods.'

Tuesday, Jan. 5. — After dinner to-day, Mr G. extraordinarily gay. He had bought a present of silver for his wife. She tried to guess the price, and after the manner of wives in such a case, put the figure provokingly low. Mr G. then put on the deprecating air of the tradesman with wounded feelings – and it was as capital fun as we could desire. That over, he fell to his backgammon with our host.

Wednesday, Jan. 6. — Mrs Gladstone eighty to-day! What a marvel....

Léon Say called to see Mr G. Long and most interesting conversation about all sorts of aspects of French politics, the concordat, the schools, and all the rest of it....

I am constantly struck by his solicitude for the well-being and right doing of Oxford and Cambridge – 'the two eyes of the country.' This connection between the higher education and the general movement of the national mind engages his profound attention, and no doubt deserves such attention in any statesman who looks beyond the mere surface problems of the day. To perceive the bearings of such matters as these, makes Mr G. a statesman of the highest class, as distinguished from men of clever expedients....

All the rest of the evening he kept us alive by a stock of infinite drolleries. A scene of a dish of over-boiled tea at West Calder after a meeting, would have made the fortune of a comedian....

Told us of a Chinese despatch which came under his notice when he was at the board of trade, and gave him food for reflection. A ship laden with grain came to Canton. The administrator wrote to the central government at Pekin to know whether the ship was to pay duty and land its cargo. The answer was to the effect that the Central Government of the Flowery Land was quite indifferent as a rule to the goings and comings of the Barbarians; whether they brought a cargo or brought no cargo was a thing of supreme unconcern. 'But this cargo, you say, is food for the people. There ought to be no obstacle to the entry of food for the people. So let it in. Your Younger Brother commends himself to you, etc. etc.'

Friday, Jan. 8. — A quiet evening. We were all rather *piano* at the end of an episode which had been thoroughly delightful. When Mr G. bade me good-night, he said with real feeling, 'More sorry than I can say that this is our last evening together at Biarritz.' He is painfully grieved to lose the sound of the sea in his ears.

Saturday, Jan. 9. — Strolled about all the forenoon. 'What a time of blessed composure it has been,' said Mr G. with a heavy sigh. The distant hills covered with snow, and the voice of the storm gradually swelling. Still the savage fury of the sea was yet some hours off, so we had to leave Biarritz without the spectacle of Atlantic rage at its fiercest....

Notes by Morley

1   On some other occasion he set this against Macaulay's praise of a passage in Barrow.
2   'Ask not, mariner, whose tomb I am here, but be thing own fortune a kinder sea.'
3   'I have not succeeded in hitting on the passage in the *History*.'
4   *Translations by Lyttelton and Gladstone*, p. 166.

APPENDIX IV

GLADSTONE AS SEEN BY
FRANK HARRISON HILL

Strangers in the Gallery, if they are really strangers and not habitual loungers who pass by that name, have one unanimous curiosity, when they have taken in the scene about them, when they have overcome their disappointment at the homely and ill-furnished apartment in which more powerful rulers than the Roman Senate govern a greater Empire than that of Rome; when they have been disabused of their impression that the Sergeant-at-Arms is the Speaker, and have had the three wigged-and-gowned gentlemen at the table explained; when these preliminary adjustments of the organisation to the environment have been effected – their eyes with one accord look, and their tongues with one accord inquire, for Mr Gladstone. Is he in the House? Where is he? Where is he? The absorption of interest is intelligible and inevitable. Mr Gladstone is the most famous of modern Englishmen. But he is something more than that. He is a piece of history living and moving among us. A new generation awakening to political curiosity looks upon him with something of the feeling with which it would gaze on Chatham, or Pitt, or Fox, if some power, cheating the magic of the grave, could bring them with the habit, the movements and speech of their daily life. While Mr Gladstone yet sits in the House of Commons, his statue might appropriately take its place with the effigies of the great Parliament men which line St Stephen's Hall. St Stephen's Hall is the old St Stephen's Chapel, or rather stands upon its site – Mr Gladstone of living men has sat in the chamber in which, from the reign of Edward VI to and well into that of William IV, the Commons have met. His voice has been heard within the walls which have echoed to the tones of Pitt and of Fox, and Chatham, as yet uncoroneted, and Walpole, Hampden and Falkland, of Pym and Wentworth, of Cecil and Bacon. He took his seat in the House of Commons in January 1833, in the first session of the first reformed Parliament. The House of Commons was burned down in October 1834, an event which fancy might take as symbolical as the ending of a political era. The old House had fulfilled its mission, and a new habitation was required for the new spirit which had entered into the British Constitution. Mr Gladstone is thus the remaining link which connects through their material structures the Parliaments of the Tudors and the Stuarts, of the Commonwealth and the Restoration, of the Revolution and the Hanoverian Settlements, with the reformed and re-reformed, and once again reformed House of Commons of the present and the immediately preceding reign. No wonder the feeling with which he is regarded is a curious blending of many feelings. He seems the relic of a great past, the embodiment of the traditions of the English Parliament from the time of the Reformation to that of the Reform Bill, the link which connects the heroes and the struggles of three centuries with the strifes in which for two generations he has played a foremost part, and the troubles which an old age less fortunate than his youth and prime seems to be preparing for his country. But we are keeping Mr Gladstone and the House of Commons and the strangers in the Gallery waiting. It is a little before question time. A perceptible stir, a turning of the heads of his colleagues towards the space behind the Speaker's chair, a slight shifting of their seats by Sir William Harcourt and Mr John Morley, so as to leave a gap between them, and opposite the Ministerial box on the table; and Mr Gladstone enters, with rapid step, erect, and looking round him as in invitation of the 'reception' which is as dear to actors in St Stephen's as to actors on any other stage, and which seldom fails him. The massive head, with its eager eyes, and prominent features, and deep lines of labour and passion, seems almost to dwarf the spare and shrunken form which supports it. Mr Gladstone is too much of a dramatic artist to have Mr Disraeli's somewhat theatrical weakness for walking solemnly on great occasions along the whole length of the floor from under the Strangers' Gallery in a stately 'procession of one.' He is not restrained by that curious shamefacedness which clung to Sir Robert Peel to the last day of his Parliamentary life, and which gave a sort of maidenly coyness to his demeanour which did not quit him till he was fairly settled in his seat.

Mr Gladstone has the faculty noticeable in most great actors, though they may come on the scenes from some obscure and distant point, of filling the stage, as the phrase runs, and catching the eye of the spectators. An unobtrusive entrance is dramatically the most effective. That the great man should be discovered by the eyes that are watching for him is far more telling than an ostentatious obtrusion of himself. The manner in which Mr Gladstone drops into his seat, adjusts his papers, and turns to converse with his colleagues on either hand, is so very natural as to seem almost unnatural. It suggests stage business, and Mr Gladstone at once both to be himself and to be acting himself. This is not strange. For more than sixty years, Mr Gladstone has spent the greatest part of his waking hours in the view and hearing of the world. He lives in the presence of the public as under the eye of his Great Taskmaster, which never slumbers nor sleeps. His demeanour in the House of Commons, his gestures and changes of his posture, and play of countenance, though not addressed to the lookers-on - that would be a blunder like that of a mugging actor - are yet shaped, and informed and controlled by the consciousness of hundreds of watchful eyes and commenting tongues. Mr Gladstone's by-play, when he has no direct part in the speech or business of the scene, is the result of careful study, and is worth studying.

The same mastery of the business of the Parliamentary stage is shown when Mr Gladstone rises to answer questions. The courteous leaning over the table, the deprecatory or explanatory gestures, the easily and nervously inflected tones, the occasional pleasantry, rather good-humoured and jocose than humorous or witty, are models of the conversational manner in Parliament. A great actor can do not only the highest but the lowest work of his art better than others. If he had simply to deliver a message or hand in a letter, he would do it as if it had not been done before.

Garrick, as the messenger bringing the news of the advance of Birnham Wood, would draw attention from most Macbeths. Something like that is literally true of Mr Gladstone. As he stands below the bar, with a Bill, or the counterfeit presentment of a Bill, which the House has just ordered to be brought in, or with a message from Her Majesty, and in reply to the Speaker's summons advances with it to the chair, the purely formal business is done with a grace and propriety which is not in everybody's reach, as is conspicuous when other Ministers hurry or stumble along like schoolboys advancing to their headmaster's desk to receive the reward of merit on prize-day. Another art Mr Gladstone possesses to perfection. 'She will be an actress,' said Mlle Mars of Rachel; 'she knows how to listen.' This is, we believe, held on the mimic stage to be the very beginning of the actor's art. In most cases, according to ordinary play-going experience, it is a beginning which is never made. The attendants on the scenes are usually remarkable for not attending. The humble confidants of either sex are obviously entirely uninterested in the startling or thrilling communications which are made to them. They roll their eyes round the house, much more concerned at anything which may be going on among the audience than with the sorrows, or joys, the perplexities or the projects of the leading gentleman or lady. They survey the front critically, computing possibly the take of the evening, and discriminating the relative proportions of paper and pay; or they stare into the pit or gallery trying to pick out some friend to whom they have been allowed to give a free pass, and with whom they have a tavern engagement when the curtain is down.

Mr Gladstone is a consummate master of the art of listening. It is as good as a play to observe him. He has his various manners. To a Parliamentary beginner, he good-naturedly turns with an air of curiosity and of what must often prove embarrassing attentiveness, with hand to the side of his head, forming an improvised ear-trumpet, and his whole attitude exhibiting a pleased receptiveness. The same posture is assumed on the occasional intrusion into the debate of an habitually silent supporter, who is to be encouraged into the belief that he is making a valuable contribution to the discussion, and who is afterwards to receive the assurance of Mr Gladstone's regret, shared, he is confident, by the whole House, that he does not more frequently give him and it the benefit of his opinions. But the real debates are, of course, with the Front Bench opposite, or with those scattered fragments of his own former Front Bench which are collected together, under Mr Chamberlain, in the back seats below the gangway.

Mr Gladstone's first attitude as Mr Balfour, let us say, rises is different. He seems to sink into himself, in an unnatural quietude, more threatening to those who know him than his habitual restlessness. He is all eye and ear and concentrated attention, as hushed in grim repose, behind his shirt collar, which seems touched up to listen, instinct with life, he waits his evening prey. Signs of uneasiness are exhibited. Mr Gladstone begins to move restlessly. The lounging attitude in which he seems to recline unequally poised on his cervical vertebrae is exchanged for a bolt upright position, which would seem preparatory, as it was sometimes, to Mr Gladstone's getting to his feet to administer the retort which is pressing for escape from behind the bulwark of his teeth. Usually he is content, however, to whisper it into the ears of some deferential colleague. But the period of restraint is now over, and the speech of the adversary has to be delivered to an accompaniment of *sotto voce* reply occasionally propelled like a missile across the table, to his direct address, after the fashion of a shot across a ship's bows, intended to bring him to, or constraining him to change his course and go upon another tack. Ordinarily, however, Mr Gladstone is content to carry on a private debate of his own before his colleagues in contemplation of the time when he will have the whole House for his audience. The conversation, or rather monologue, sometimes becomes so animated and contumacious, that the orator in possession stops as Pitt did, when on a now historic occasion, which shows that Front benches succeed and resemble each other, and were a hundred years ago pretty much what they are now, he paused until Nestor should have adjusted the dispute between Agamemnon and Achilles. For the moment the 'appeal to the right honourable gentleman to give me his attention' is successful. But the whispered comments begin again, and are accompanied and illustrated by movements of impatience or incredulity, gestures of surprise or indignation. Often a true description would be the speech by Mr Balfour, the gesticulation by Mr Gladstone. It is the triumph of political pantomime. 'We understood,' wrote Dr John Donne in his funeral elegy on the death of Mistress Drury:

> 'We understood her by her right; her pure and eloquent blood
> Spoke in her cheeks and so distinctly wrought,
> That one might almost say her body thought.'

These lines are not, perhaps, in the strict letter applicable to Mr Gladstone; but still it may be said that 'we understand him by his right.' His whole body debates in every part of it, from head to foot, his mobile features, vibrating and pointing finger, theatening arm, restless figure, turning now this way, now that, now erect at the table, now prone over it. To Mr Gladstone, as he himself has said, debating is a wrestle with a single antagonist, or with a succession of antagonists, one up and down, and usually in the issue more of them down than up. His attitude, as the speech to which he is to reply draws to a close, is often that of a couchant animal, drawn together for a spring, and he leaps from his lair in a manner which enables the spectator to understand Mr Disraeli's expression of thankfulness for the solid piece of furniture which separated them, and which was destined to receive the resounding blows that seemed in Mr Gladstone's intention to be aimed at the person of his antagonist. Sometimes, however, the mere fact of getting upon his legs has a chastening effect upon the orator. The nervous excitement, which while silence, a relative silence, was imposed upon him, worked itself out in gestures and shrugs and facial play, in the muscles of countenance and limb, and in half-audible comments, like the mutterings which prelude a storm that is about to break, flows in a calmer course when it finds a vent in the natural channel of continuous speech.

Mr Gladstone rises, straightens himself, puts his hands behind his back, and folds them together, as if each were in the custody of the other, as a security against outbreak. He takes a sobering glance at the Speaker, the visible and outward sign of the inward spiritual grace of self-restraint and reciprocal courtesy, to whom by Parliamentary form the opening words of his speech are addressed, as indeed by a fiction never translated into fact the whole of every speech is supposed to be. He begins in easy and natural conversational tones, animated but not turbulent or violent, increasing in vivacity as he goes on: the erect figure becomes mobile, swaying now this way, now that, something after the manner of a preacher essaying to bring the whole of his congregation under the influence of his looks and voice. Gradually one hand escapes from the keeping of its guardian hand, and begins to play with expressive and illustrative gestures. As it returns to its old position, or rests on the table or droops b the speaker's side, the other comes forward *le même jeu*, as the French stage direction has it. On rare occasions, when business is non-contentious, and Mr Gladstone has only to give shape and reason to the acquiescent opinions and foregone conclusion of the whole House, or the great majority of it, the stream of his speech does not burst its banks. It flows well between them, strong without rage. Usually, however, this prelusive calm is short-lived. Ordinarily his business is not to keep the House of one mind, but to excite one side of the House against the other. Then Mr Gladstone lets himself loose. His voice becomes loud and denunciatory. He bends across the table, thrusting his face as nearly as the space between the two Front Benches allows into the face of his antagonist, too much after the manner of a provocative street scold. His blows are literally delivered from the shoulder, not at but in the direction of his adversaries. If the opponent of the moment is in a remoter part of the House, he turns to him with gestures of distant defiance which seem to challenge him to come down and have it out, or to warn him of what would be his fate if he did. Mr Gladstone's tone and demeanour are those of a man in a sort of frenzy, and it is impossible to witness them without pain at a certain unseemliness in the spectacle. Mr Gladstone, instead of outliving his *Sturm und Drang* period, has carried it into his eighty-fifth year; the serenity and brightness of a Lapland night, in which Wordsworth saw the image of a noble age, are not his. The tumult and storm of a *Walpurgisnacht* are a truer symbol of his mood. It is not probable that Mr Gladstone is carried away by a fervour which he cannot control. He is a consenting party to the passion by which he is abducted. He has instigated and arranged the seeming violence. His excitement is voluntary. It is self-produced. It does not so much inspire as it is the creation of the tones and gestures which seem to express it. It is a common truth of psychology, and a fact which may be observed every day, that by assuming the signs of any emotion, the emotion itself is generated. The operation is reciprocal. The signs naturally express the emotion when it already exists. They can call it into existence when it is absent and give it almost any degree of force. The phenomenon known as working oneself into a passion is familiar to everybody, in some cases unhappily through inner experience, in others by common observation. By loud tones and violent gestures, setting of the teeth and knitting of the brows, a man, or perhaps more frequently a woman, can bring himself or herself into any mood of passion which he or she desire, and into any degree of that mood. Actors know this well. Before rushing on as Shylock in the Tubal scene, Macready was in the habit of swaying himself backwards and forwards with vehement gestures, endeavouring to generate the proper mental excitement by bodily disturbance. Mr Gladstone's passion in debate is in a great degree of this physical origin. It is real, but it is produced artificially and with intention. It is a phenomenon as much of the animal as of the moral nature, as the lion is said to inspirit himself for fight by vigorously lashing himself with his own tail, and as the gorilla advances to the combat bellowing and beating his breast. Mr Gladstone's tones, we are sometimes told, thrill and vibrate his whole person, in his more exalted moods tremulous with conviction. The words describe an actor and not a thinker. This performer is said to spar, this other to lack conviction, according as he throws himself entirely, or fails entirely to throw himself, into his part. It applies also to the professional advocate who can produce in himself a temporary and superficial belief in the justice of a cause which he knows to be iniquitous.

Imagination is said to be a temporary belief, and the orator and the debater no doubt, unless they are very sedulously on the watch against its illusions, may surrender themselves as completely to its hallucinations as the actor or the advocate. Conviction, however, in the only sense in which it can be honourably used of this statesman, is not a thing of this kind. It shows itself not in the tumult but in the calmness of the mind. It is an affair of reason and not of passion. It is tranquil, by its very intensity. True strength, whether of conviction or of anything else, shows itself in quietness. Mr Gladstone's excitement is the result of his strenuous efforts to work himself into a belief that he believes what in the inner recesses of his mind he is conscious of only half believing. This misgiving is at the bottom of his anger with his opponents, his vigorous rating at them. Their refusal to be persuaded reflects back upon him an uneasy and irritated sense of his own suppressed and evidently overborne doubts. 'The man,' said the often-quoted clergyman, 'who is not convinced by these arguments, must be a villain indeed.' 'Villains indeed' is the category in which Mr Gladstone places all his antagonists whom he cannot set down as fools or to whom he is unable to impute ignorance. 'Dishonest or imperfectly informed' is said to be the dilemma which he charitably provides. The fact that all his censures upon their present state of mind are censures upon his past state of mind does not weight with him. He dismisses his past self, after the manner of Mr Brinnay's casuistical hero: 'Get you behind the man that I am, you man that I used to be,' and with more success than Martin Pelph, whose past self had an inconvenient and embarrassing way of entangling itself with his present self in a manner from which Mr Gladstone is wholly free.

Another and not a pleasant feature of Mr Gladstone's eloquence may plausibly be assigned to the same origin. The frequency and – the phrase cannot be spared – the levity of his appeals to the Divine name shock men of reverent mind. Mr Wordy, the great historian, thought that Providence was on the side of the Tories. The much greater Mr Wordy, the orator and statesman, affirms with emphasis and iteration that Providence is on the side of his party. God is the God of the Gladstonians, and if He has not left Himself altogether without witness among the Conservatives and Liberal-Unionists, theirs is the greater guilt for not heeding the warnings of His interpreter and prophet. Imperfect conviction dictates Mr Gladstone's attempts to overbear his own judgment by excited declamation, and to shelter himself from his own misgivings by imputing a sinister bias to his adversaries and a kind of divine mission to himself. The inner assurance is wanting, and its place is supplied by these outer proofs, which involve, of course, an enormous begging of the question.

Another characteristic of Mr Gladstone's language, his exuberant verbosity, admits in part of the same explanation. His word-spinning weaves for him a robe in which he hides himself from himself. Clear conviction and steady purpose express themselves in brief and lucid speech. Tacitus's celebrated description of eloquence, as rendered in Pitt's almost equally celebrated translation of it: 'It is with eloquence as a flame, it requires fuel to feed it, motion to excite it, and it brightens as it burns,' does not apply in its last clause to Mr Gladstone's oratory: it does not brighten as it burns. The light-bearing and the heat-bearing rays of the sun are different, and in proportion as the heat is greater, the light is less, while the converse holds good. Mr Gladstone's oratory is calorific, as Mr Balfour's is essentially circumforaneous: 'Ex fumo dare lucem' might be the motto of the one; 'De luce dare fumum' that of the other. ('To give light out of smoke' 'To give smoke out of light'.) The scale of Mr Gladstone's sentences is, however, only on the scale of his speeches. Whatever his rank among the masters of Parliamentary eloquence, he has never had, and probably never will have, any rival as a master of largiloquence. After one of the elder Pitt's speeches, he was saluted by the people outside, as he left the House, with enthusiastic cries of 'Three hours and a half.' 'Three hours and a half.' Lord Chesterfield narrating the incident in a letter to his son *avec empressement*: 'It is impossible for a man to speak well for three hours and a half.' Modern criticism, debauched by bad examples, would, we fear, be inclined to make a change of one little word in this sentence, and would say: 'It is impossible for a man to speak well in three hours and a half.' Mr Gladstone's long-speaking is the result of a circuitous and involved habit of mind. He does not approach his subject in a direct line, but winds about it in strange circumgyrations, threading endless mazes though not lost in them, and so approaching the goal as to mark the fact that he is aiming at. Traversing so much more ground than is necessary, he is perforce longer in getting over it than a speaker would be whose single purpose was himself to get, and to carry his hearers by the shortest path and with the least loss of time to their journey's end. Here we may, without, perhaps, unduly straining the interpretation, attribute Mr Gladstone's roundabout courses to a roundabout habit of mind, indisposed to face his mind directly and to take the shortest cut to it, but preferring to creep towards it, along wandering by-ways. This defect has grown upon Mr Gladstone as the garrulity natural to age has been added to his aboriginal sin of long-windedness. It is amusing, by the way, to find Mr Gladstone in his *Studies of Homer* censuring Priam for being in his old age prone in war-time, as before in peace, to speak too often and too long, at least in the opinion of younger members of the Trojan assembly.

$$\text{'}\Omega, \gamma\acute{\epsilon}\rho o\nu\ a\grave{\iota}\epsilon\acute{\iota}\ \tau o\iota\ \mu\hat{\upsilon}\theta o\iota\ \phi\acute{\iota}\lambda o\grave{\iota}\ \ddot{a}\kappa\rho\iota\tau o\acute{\iota}\ \epsilon\grave{\iota}\sigma\iota\nu,$$
$$\Omega\varsigma\ \pi o\tau'\ \dot{\epsilon}\pi'\ \epsilon\grave{\iota}\rho\eta\nu\acute{\eta}\varsigma.$$

('Old man, you always find pleasure in unending talk, as you did in peacetime.')*   (*Iliad*, Book II, 796-7)

The argument from verbose and involved speech to the lack of clear and definite opinion, and from passion to the want of reasoned assurance of truth, though morally content is not in itself demonstrative. Conviction, however, to parody Chatham's remark, is a plant of slow growth in aged minds. It is a plant still more slowly eradicated. When we find a man of eighty years throwing away to-day the opinions which he professed yesterday, and ready to throw away to-morrow those which he professes to-day, it is impossible to resist the conclusion that he does not know what it is to be really convinced of anything. Caprice or a convenient opportunism may impose themselves upon him as openness of mind, and obstinate self-will may pass itself off as steady belief.

Mr Gladstone's convictions are those of an earnest and imaginative actor, who for the moment, in the character which he assumes, has the conviction with which on one day Salvini as Othello springs at the throat of Iago, and on another day the conviction with which as Iago he spins his webs of intrigue round his dupes.

Mr Gladstone's own theory of oratory throws more light, we are disposed to

---

* Hill got the quotation wrong, and the reference.

think, upon his own characteristics as an orator, than upon the art of which he has been the most successful practitioner of the past generation. The following passage occurs in his *Studies of Homer* (vol. III, p. 107):

'Poets of modern times,' he says, 'have composed great works in ages that stopped their ears against them. *Paradise Lost* does not represent the time of Charles the Second nor *The Excursion* the first decade of the present century. The case of the orator is entirely different. His work from its very inception is inextricably mixed up with practice. It is cast in the mould offered to him by the mind of his hearers. It is an influence principally received from his audience, so to speak, in vapour which he passes back upon them as a flood. The sympathy and concurrence of his time is with his own mind joint author of his work; he cannot follow or frame ideals, his choice is to be what his age will have been, what it requires in order to be moved by him, or not to be moved at all.'

It might be fanciful to trace in these words Mr Gladstone's own conscious *Apologia pro vita sua*. But probably in those deeper and subconscious regions of the mind, in which, as in subterraneous springs, lie the real sources of character, it had a self-excusatory origin. We venture to pronounce it an ignoble and untruthful view of the orator's art and function. If it does not convert him into a demagogue it is because he is demagogued, if one may be allowed to coin a word. He is not δημαγωγός, but δημαγωγούμενος. ('He is not appealing to the people, but being controlled by them.')

This is not the place to discuss Mr Gladstone's theory of the relation of the poet to the age in which he lives, and of which, according to Mr Gladstone, he may be entirely independent. We may leave him to settle that question with M. Taine, only remarking that he seems to confound the time of Charles II with the Court of Charles II, and reminding him that there were elements in the former which were not represented in the latter, and of which Milton's poem was the ennobled embodiment. So with the 'excursion' and its relation to the first decade of the present century. The fact is that every great work of art, and not merely great oratic achievements, are the joint productions of the author and of the age in which he lives. It depends on himself what are the elements which he will select from the time in which he lives. According to his choice of character he will be a Milton or a Dryden; he will write 'excursions' or 'Don Juans.' The same freedom of choice is left to the orator, and the noblest and most durable monuments of oratic greatness have been often clothed in words of warning, rebuke, protest and contradiction, and not of sympathy and concurrence. From the time of Demosthenes, downwards to that of Mr Bright, there have been conquests over hostile or indifferent opinion, which they have boldly confronted, or defeats as noble as victory. There have been incidents in Mr Gladstone's own career which are in contradiction with his theory and general practice. It is not necessary for an orator to have the sympathy and concurrence of his audience or his time, but he must have its respect. It is not necessary that he should follow it: he may leave it.

Instead of being its slave he may be its master. It is not true that he must be what his age will have him: he may go far to make his age what he would have it. He may be a piece of Parliamentary mechanism, a condenser for converting into water what it receives as vapour, originating nothing and giving back in one form only what it has received in another. But he may be more than this. In Mr Gladstone's view the orator is simply an echo. He may be a voice, he may be only an interpreter, but he may also be an originator. Mr Gladstone holds good only if oratory is conceived simply as an instrument of personal ambition, of popular or Parliamentary centreship, as a means of winning place and power.

This explanation throws light on the limitations of Mr Gladstone's oratorical faculty. There is nothing of direct vision in his speeches. He does not, like Demosthenes, march with rapid steps straight onwards to an object which he sees clearly before him, levelling the obstacles which he finds in his path. Mr Gladstone is guided rather by a delicate sense of touch than by sight. His oratory reminds one of a man feeling his way guided by an exquisite tactile sensibility through tortuous passages and a crowd of objects over which it surely seems that he must trip, which by the mere atmospheric pressure which they convey or interrupt, warns infallibly of their presence, and enables him to keep clear of them. This physical phenomenon, which everyone must have noticed in persons blind from birth, has its counterpart in Mr Gladstone, who from the moment of his political nativity has been blind to principles. This, to use his own metaphor, which had a deeper truth than he saw, or would allow, is the practised Parliamentary hand, and not the clear and single eye, full of light. His involved and circuitous sentences, swaying now this way, now that, turning in upon themselves, trying as it were first one path and then the other, and apparently, when they begin, leaving himself as much in doubt how and where they will end as his hearers are, are characteristic of this habit of mind. Mr Gladstone's oratory has been described with some truth, but more indulgence, as that of a man thinking aloud. A better phrase, perhaps, would have been 'inventing as he goes on.' What, however, does even the politer description imply? It means that the speaking and the thinking begin together: that his language is not the outer and visible symbol shaped by causes superior to the accidents of the moment, of long-mature inward convictions, but the hastily caught-up vesture with which the nakedness of new suggestions is clothed. Hence results that remarkable poverty of his speeches in everything which can be called thought, and in those felicitous expressions which remain the permanent embodiment of some idea, those aphorisms which take their place, like the best lines of the best poets in our language, and become a part of our literature. Of these the richest legacy that any orator has bequeathed to any nation is to tbe found in the speeches of Burke. But at intervals they relieve and refresh like oases the long desert tracks of the harangues of much inferior. Lord John Russell in his best moods is an example whose rooted convictions have had time to burst into the appropriate foliage and flower. The phrases which are currently quoted from Mr Gladstone's speeches, 'advancing by leaps and bounds,' 'approaching within measurable distance,' 'outside the sphere of practical politics,' 'up in a balloon,' 'an old Parliamentary hand,' have a certain felicity and currency of slang. Mr Gladstone's eloquence, it has often been said, is to oratory, in the higher sense of the term, what improvisation is to poetry. This is almost in its terms what Byron said of Fox. The comparison, however, involves some injustice. Improvisation in poetry and improvisation in oratory do not stand upon the same level. Improvisation is the degradation of poetry or rather of the poetic form, it banishes the poetic spirit, abusing it for the display of a mechanical ingenuity, scarcely above the intellectual level of a conjuror's trick. To be able, by a process of automatic continuation and verbal association, to pour forth a long screed of rhymed and metrical sentences, more or less exactly constructed, springing from no feeling and appealing to none, is an accomplishment not much superior to the cheapjack. There are no doubt political improvisators of this kind who hold forth with an incessant dribble of words, words, words, without logical beginning, middle or end. But in another sense improvisation, so far from being the degradation of oratory, is the essential condition of one of its most useful, and common, though not its noblest forms. The orator, as Mr Gladstone conceives and has described him, in the passage which has been already quoted from his *Studies in Homer*, is in his nature an improviser. His skill consists in instantaneously adapting himself to the changing moods of his audience. He is something less than the creature of his time, the product of his age, as Mr Gladstone describes him. He is the creature of the hour and the place, and will be a different creature at another hour, and in another at another hour, or even in the same place. This is true not merely of his speech as a whole, and of the period as a whole during which it is being delivered. It is true of every part of his speech, almost literally of every sentence of it, which is a new birth of the moment in which it originates. It echoes the changing feelings of its audience and becomes more highly wrought or flags, is persistent, in the same mood, or fluctuates. There is a philosophic theory of the universe which resolves its continuance with a series of instantaneous and incessantly renewed acts of creation. The orator, of the class of which we are speaking, whom Mr Gladstone's practice embodies, and of whom his theory alone takes account, illustrates this principle. The creative impulse from which his speech springs sentence by sentence, is conveyed moment by moment from the varying mood of the audience to the sensitive intelligence of the orator. He is not propelled by an earnest impulse from the starting-point to the goal. He obeys a succession of impulses from without, now hastening, now slackening, now diverting his course, according as they are strained or relaxed or waver. He sees much to invigorate in them the feeling which he receives from them, in part creating the force which he obeys, and leading his audience by dint of fast fettering them in the direction which they have indicated.

APPENDIX V

LORD TOLLEMACHE AND HIS ANECDOTES

' Θάνατος δέ τοι αὐτῷ
'Αβληχρὸς μάλα τοῖος ἐλευσεται, ὅς κέ σε πέφνῃ
Γηραι ὕπο λιπαρῷ ἀρημένον· ἀμφὶ δε λαοί
'Ολβιοι ἔσσονται.' *

It is not my purpose to say much about my father, either as a politician or as a landlord. He regarded the Reform Bill of 1832 as, at best, a necessary evil. He even thought that, if Peel had disfranchised every corrupt borough and transferred the Members to large constituencies, such as Manchester, the extension of the franchise might have been delayed, if not averted. He was one of the fifty or sixty Members who, at the very last division, opposed the repeal of the Corn Laws. He continued a Protectionist to the end; and on this as on other matters he had the courage of his opinions. Indeed, in allusion to old cartoon in *Punch*, he used jocularly to call himself one of the fifty cannon balls which nothing could melt. He held that Free Trade would have speedily ruined British agriculture, if it had not been for the discovery of gold; and he was fond of quoting a high commercial authority as having said that this discovery 'had given the greatest stimulus to trade that the world had ever known.' He talked the matter over with that charming and accomplished old man, the late Mr George Norman, whose opinion carried great weight in matters of political economy and finance, and whose name is familiar to the readers of *The Life of George Grote*. Mr Norman indirectly confirmed my father in his opinion by telling him that the discovery of gold had raised prices as much as ten per cent; but I am bound to add that Mr Norman told me that, in his opinion, the rise of prices had done more harm than good.

One thing has always struck me about my father's rules in regard to allotments

---

* 'And thou shalt fall in a serene old age,
Painless and ripe, with nothing left to do,
While a blest people at thy gates engage
Thy [fostering] care.'
Worsley's Translation

and to the general management of his estates. When I was living under his roof thirty years ago, those somewhat arbitrary rules were thought by many landowners to be as eccentric as (to compare small things with great) the British Constitution was thought on the Continent in the last century. On the other hand, this same system has suddenly gained such a wide popularity as almost to suggest a comparison with the present popularity of our Constitution all over the world. What was the cause of this surprising change? The proximate cause seems to have been a speech delivered by Mr Chamberlain when my father was in his eightieth year, a speech which declared him to be one of the very best of English landlords, and which straightway transformed the old-fashioned Protectionist into a Radical hero. Thereupon his theory suddenly became *ex humili potens*.[1] Seeing what appeared to be its dry bones thus live, one is tempted to adapt the words of the banished Bolingbroke, and to exclaim, 'Such is the breath of *orators*.'

Other and wider causes doubtless helped on the change, causes connected with the decline of the *laissez-faire* school of political economy. Mr Norman, himself a strong adherent of that school, told me that an inquiry had been set on foot as to the comparative rate of wages on different Suffolk estates, and he believed that the labourers on my father's estate were little, if at all, better off than the labourers on other estates; the rate of wages had found its level, and the labourers on my father's estate received as much *less* from the farmers as they received *more* from the landlord. Doubtless there was some overstatement in this. At any rate, my father, when a very old man, knew nothing of the untoward investigation. But I refer to it as showing the instinctive repulsion with which some political economists of the old school would have regarded the masterful beneficience even of a model landlord. Or, to speak more precisely, a disciple of that school would pronounce Lord Tollemache's paternal landlordism (as, indeed, he could pronounce Mr Gladstone's Irish Land Act) to be a needful anomaly, perhaps, but certainly an anomaly, and to involve the assumption that political economy is a less exact science – is less of a *quod semper, quod ubique, quod omnibus*[2] – than it was once thought to be.

The above consideration may be further illustrated by a personal remark, which I make with some reluctance, but which may be thought suggestive. One of my father's neighbours was that very remarkable man, Mr Charles Austin. It was partly under his guidance that I broke loose from my hereditary politics, and became a staunch Whig and an upholder of what is now called Individualism. My father, whose view of the *Patria potestas*[3] might have found favour with Brutus or Camillus, was wont to rate me soundly for my 'harum-scarum' notions. But the Liberal Party has since changed its front, and Individualism is giving place to State Socialism; and, at the same time, it has been my good or bad fortune to continue in the main loyal to the principles of Ricardo –

> 'though fallen on evil days,
> On evil days though fallen, and evil tongues.'

The odd result of all this was that my father, at the end of his active and useful life, seemed to be in some respects less out of sympathy with modern Liberalism than I was.

Some of my readers will remember that my father drove almost, if not quite, the last curricle in London – one of those not very safe, but comfortable and picturesque, carriages which seemed to take one bodily into the England of Miss Austen. The mention of these old-world conveyances indirectly recalls a quaint remark made three years ago by a French *garçon*, who wore an antique dress, and showed me, in the so-called Rue de la Bastille, a full-sized model of a restaurant of the last century: 'Il n'y a rien de changé, *sauf le personnel!*'

In early youth my father was extraordinarily active. So much so, indeed, that, in a race of one hundred yards, he twice beat the champion runner of England. In relating this, however, he was careful to explain that he was several years younger than the champion, who had passed his prime. In later life his chief amusement was driving four-in-hand; and, on at least one occasion, he drove his four chestnut horses when he was over eighty. When I congratulated him n this achievement, he gave the characteristic explanation, 'I had a young fool of a coachman who didn't know how to drive; so I had to teach him. I found it hard work to get on the box; but, when I was once hoisted up, I was all right.' Alas! how often the thought of him who has been taken from us – a muscular Puritan, if ever there was one – has tempted me with all reverence to exclaim: '*Pater mi, pater mi, currus Israel, et auriga ejus!*'[4] His unusual strength and agility were inherited from his father, Admiral Tollemache: *il chassoit de race*. During the peace of Amiens the Admiral was at Calais, playing the pocketless game which the French call billiards. As he was making a stroke, a French bully nudged his arm. A repetition of the offence having shown it to be no accident, he threw the Frenchman out of the window; and then, warned by the landlord, ran for his life. The impetuous temper thus shown devolved in full measure on his son, as might be proved by numerous examples.

The following adventure of his youth will astonish those who are conversant only with the stately Evangelicalism of his declining years. Once when he was travelling with a friend, his dressing-case was stolen. The friend had seen a suspicious-looking stranger standing by; and from his description the authorities of Scotland Yard identified the man with a noted thief, but there was no legal proof, and the affair was dropped. At the next Derby, my father, pointing out a horse to the same friend, said that, if he were to bet, he would back that horse. A stranger, overhearing him, offered him odds of 25 to 1 against it in five-pound notes. My father took the bet, and was much surprised when his friend whispered in his ear that the stranger was no other than the thief. The horse won, and the miscreant had to disgorge more than the value of what he had stolen. So that, in this case, '*Ridebat* plenus *coram latrone viator.*'[5]

My father, before appointing an incumbent to one of his numerous livings, made the noble resolution that (as he expressed it) he would select, not merely a good man, but the very best he could find. It happened on a Sunday afternoon that he attended the church of one of his nominees – the opposite end of the social-scale being represented by an infirm peasant whom I will call John Martin. The eloquent preacher impressed on his hearers that (to speak broadly) there will be no reserved seats in Heaven: 'All of you, my brethren, from you, Lord Tollemache, down to you, John Martin, will stand side by side before the judgement-seat of God!' The patron, I understand, was asleep.

And now, having furnished a few facts about the non-agricultural life of this most painstaking and exemplary landlord, I am sorely tempted to pass on at once to the anecdotes which he told about others; for I know that – just as Wellington held a great victory to be an evil second only to a great defeat – even so, the most delicate task for a son, next to speaking of his father's defects, is to speak of his father's virtues. But it would be unfilial, and might give rise to misconstruction, if I were to forego all expression of feeling. Briefly, then, I will apply to the present subject a quotation from *The Lady of the Lake:* –

> 'His ready speech flowed fair and free,
> In phrase of gentlest courtesy;
> Yet seemed that tone and gesture bland
> Less used to sue than to command.'

These lines express a part of what I feel, but only a part. An original picture – I think the only one – of *the* Lord Falkland used to belong to our family. The late Lord Falkland begged my father, as an old friend, to let him bury this memorial of his ancestor; and my father – wishing, as he expressed it, to do as he would be done by – consented to the proposal, and replaced the original picture by a copy. This may be taken as a typical instance of the kindness, nay, the exceeding great kindness, which was often shown by him. I want, however, to lay stress on the fact that he had (so to say) *les qualités de ses défauts*; if he had been less *masterful*, his work might have been less *masterly*. In fact, he might be roughly described as three parts Sir Roger de Coverley and one part Cardinal Richelieu. 'Roughly,' I say, for assuredly he had virtues of a kind which neither of these had. One great virtue he derived from his Evangelicalism. He was liberal alike of sympathy and of money to orthodox Dissenters; and it may have been in consequence of this sympathy, or rather of its religious basis, that, though himself an aristocrat to the backbone, he was remarkably tolerant of the class of persons whose real worth is veiled by social shortcomings, and whose aspirations are less defective than their aspirates. Let me say, too, that, when I read of the few philanthropic French *seigneurs* of the last century, I am instinctively reminded of him. Is it unbecoming for a son to add concerning his father that the setting, so to say, was worthy of the gem – that there was in him, absolutely when in his prime, relatively when in extreme old age, a dignity of presence and of bearing, *Gratior et pulchro veniens in corpore virtus*?[6] This manifold combination of qualities has led to the result that, though for many years he and I had scarce a taste or a thought in common, and though he was neither politician nor orator nor philosopher nor scholar, I believe him to have been the grandest specimen of a country gentleman that our generation has seen or is likely to see ...

Between the years 1858 and 1866 my father used often to take me as his son into one of the seats under the gallery of the House of Commons. Naturally, however, the better the debate, the harder it was to get me in. Perhaps this is the reason why the speeches have left so little impression on my memory. The quaintest thing that I remember hearing was a comparison made by Bernal Osborne between Pius IX and Lord Palmerston: 'Both began as reformers. Both withdrew their reforms. *Non possumus*[7] became the motto of the one, as of the other. And now what is the result? The one is defended by French bayonets, and *the other by Conservative votes*.'

At my special request I was taken to hear Mr Goschen second the address on the Queen's Speech. I afterwards told Hayward how much Mr Goschen's speech had impressed me. Hayward was also impressed, but characteristically added: 'The thing that most struck me in connection with it was the remark made by Lord Hotham, that he had never before known a young member make so long a speech without once apologising for trespassing on the patience of the House. One always likes to have a *foolometer*.' It was, I think, Sydney Smith who coined this ungracious word. I have sometimes thought that such a word as *Philistino-meter* or *fashionometer* would be convenient and comparatively inoffensive. Be that as it may, foolometry is the one science in which the wise have much to learn from the unwise. And it is a very useful science...

Though my father had little sympathy with Brougham, he believed him to be a man of genuine convictions, while he held, in a modified form, the opinion of Miss Martineau and Walter Bagehot that Brougham's great rival, Copley, was always an advocate, and was without strong convictions. In confirmation of this view, Charles Austin related a fact illustrative of the bitter indignation which prevailed among the Whigs when Copley, like another Stafford, suddenly 'ratted' and turned Tory. So extreme was this resentment that Denman told his servant that, if his old friend called, he was not to be admitted. In spite of the servant the future Lord Lyndhurst made his way to the door of Denman's chambers and shouted from outside, 'Let me at least beg that, if you are asked about my change of opinions, you will say that it was honest.' 'If I am asked about your change of opinions,' was the reply from within, 'I will say that *you say* that it was honest.'

It may not be amiss to subjoin one of my father's anecdotes about Ham House, which is the seat of the elder branch of our family, and is familiar by name to the readers of Evelyn and Walpole. Sixty years ago this 'most mournfully fascinating of places' belonged to Louisa, Countess of Dysart in her own right, who, like some other of our kinsfolk, might have taken *Sit pro ratione voluntas*[8] as a motto. One day this original lady sent an express to the first surgeon in London, begging him to come to her at once. He reached Ham in the middle of the night; and, on asking what accident had befallen her ladyship, was told that her lapdog had broken its leg!

It seems to me only the other day (*ut vidi! ut memini!*[9]) when my father used to pack some fourteen persons (including his young children and grandchildren) into a huge four-in-hand carriage, nicknamed the 'village,' and to drive us to Richmond; and from Richmond we rowed up the river to Ham. In one of these patriarchal trips it was casually mentioned that the notorious Duke of Lauderdale lived at Ham House, and that a room is shown where the Cabal Ministry used to meet. On hearing this, an eminent orator, who was of the party, repeated the following satire on the Duke, the authorship of which I have failed to trace:–

> 'He was not a Jew, for he ate of the swine,
> He was not a Turk, for he drank of the wine;
> But let this inscription be writ on his grave:
> *He was not a Christian – he never forgave!*'

I quote these lines, not merely because they are at once vigorous and unfamiliar, but also because they indicate one of the besetting sins laid to the charge of our landlords as a class. The charge is not wholly without foundation. And yet, in spite of all that has been done amiss and left undone, one is wont to echo the piteous lament, *O patria, O divom domus Ilium,*[10] if one lingers for a moment on the hateful foreboding that the country gentlemen and their stately traditions, and their Church as a National Church, and all they dying embers of feudalism, nay, that the old England of Shakespeare and of Scott, will soon be as extinct as the dodo. An antidote, or perhaps a counter-irritant, to these useless regrets may be found in a strange old-world story, which my father related as true. At my old home there is an avenue of giant trees which can have changed but little during the last three centuries, and which seem to look down with lofty compassion as generation after generation of their puny owners passes from the scene. Beneath the shade of these 'monumental oaks' (as Milton would have called them) Queen Elizabeth made her way in 1561, and crossed the Helmingham drawbridge, on a visit to Sir Lionel Tollemache† with the view of standing godmother to his child. The infant died; but, fearing to disappoint Elizabeth, the parents had the dead body duly christened! The lute given by the Queen to the child's mother is still an heirloom in the family; and the drawbridge is still raised every night as it is said to have been for centuries. *Il n'y rien de changé, sauf le personnel.*‡

Notes by Tollemache

† I adopt (as Thackeray in *Esmond* adopts) the modern spelling of the surname, though probably 'Talmash' would be more correct. In the good old times surnames were spelt at random.

‡ In illustration of the age ascribed to some trees in Suffolk, my father told me the following incident about an oak near Bury St Edmund's Tradition says that St Edmund was tracked by means of wolves, that he was bound to this oak and was shot with arrows, and that by way of insult some wolves' bones were buried with his bones. Not long ago, wolves' bones were discovered near the spot; and the decaying oak having been afterwards blown down, was examined, and the barb of an arrow was found near its centre. These facts, though not conclusive, are certainly curious.

TRANSLATIONS OF LATIN

1. 'Rising to greatness from a low estate.'
2. 'What is always [believed], what is everywhere [believed], what is believed by all.'
3. 'A father's power.'
4. 'My father, my father, the chariot of Israel, and the horseman thereof.'
5. 'The traveller with *full* pockets laughed in the highwayman's face.'
6. 'And manliness more winning because it showed itself in a fair body.'
7. 'We cannot.'
8. 'Let my will count as reason.'
9. 'How I saw, how I remember.' Tollemache misquotes, mispunctuates and misunderstands.
10. 'O my country, O Ilium, home of the gods.'